HOW SWEET IT WAS

TELEVISION: A PICTORIAL COMMENTARY

By Arthur Shulman and Roger Youman

HOME SAVINGS takes pleasure in presenting you with this nostalgic review of the exciting and memorable early years of television. We hope you will enjoy reliving these great moments in entertainment as much as we enjoy bringing them to you.

Harry von Zell

Library of Congress Catalog Card Number: 66-24164
Manufactured in the United States of America
This edition published by Bonanza Books, a division of Crown Publishers, Inc., by arrangement with Shorecrest, Inc.

HX 3881

□*"Television is the educator and the communicator, the informer, the thing that can inspire and enrich man as he makes his greatest transition from what he is today into the first genuine adult human being."* —Sylvester L. Weaver

□*"Television is a triumph of equipment over people, and the minds that control it are so small that you could put them in the navel of a flea and still have enough room beside them for a network vice-president's heart."* —Fred Allen

□*"Television is the greatest single power in the hands of mortal man."* —LeRoy Collins

□*"It is a medium of entertainment which permits millions of people to listen to the same joke at the same time, and yet remain lonesome."* —T. S. Eliot

□*"Television is now recognized everywhere as a vehicle for education and information, a force to arouse and unify developing nations, and a symbol of national status and prestige that soars above the home-grown airline."* —Robert E. Kintner

□*". . . a vast wasteland."* —Newton N. Minow

□*"Well, I'd say it's pretty good, considering it's for nothing."* —Bing Crosby

□*"Some television programs are so much chewing gum for the eyes."* —John Mason Brown

□*"We are human and, given a chance, we still might create an art form of television."* —Gilbert Seldes

How Sweet It Was

ONE CAN OBTAIN as many opinions about television as there are people with eyes. No two people see it in exactly the same way. But whatever you think of television—whether you like it or loathe it or just tolerate it; whether you are grateful for it or scornful of it; whether you watch it a lot or a little—whatever your attitude is toward it, television has become a part of you.

You may not be aware of it, but up there, in that compartment of your brain where memories are stored, all sorts of strange images are stockpiled. They are greyish rectangles, sort of, but with rounded edges, and inside them are people and places and things of every description. Some of them can be recalled merely by twisting a mental dial; others lurk there patiently, waiting for an external stimulus that will pull them out of their dusty corners and into your mind's eye. These are your memories of television past.

The purpose of this book is to coax those memories out of their hiding places and bring them front and center, where you can savor them anew. The book contains more than fourteen hundred photographs, and they are populated by thousands of people. Some of them you will recognize immediately; others will be vaguely familiar; many will be total strangers. You will find programs you

INTRODUCTION

remember with affection, and others you recall with distaste; programs that lasted for years, others that disappeared after a few weeks; significant events from television's history, and trivial moments; brilliantly talented performers, and inept clods. Some of the photographs will make you smile fondly, some will make you laugh derisively, some will bring back solemn recollections, some will draw a complete blank.

Although this book is intended to be a comprehensive review of television during the past twenty years—the two decades that have passed since the medium became a commercial reality—it is not meant to be just a scholarly history. The programs and people represented here were chosen not because they were "good" or "popular" or "successful," but because each contributed, in some large or small way, to the progress of television. Theirs may not necessarily have been a beneficial contribution, just as the progress of the medium has not necessarily been in the direction of higher quality. Individually many of these pictures mean little, except to a few people; but considered cumulatively and in relation to each other, they constitute a panorama of the television scene since the late forties.

For better or for worse, in sickness and in health, this is what television has been during the past twenty years.

A Bunch of Bananas

RESPLENDENT IN BAGGY PANTS and putty nose, the comedians were in the vanguard when television arrived. Although from the beginning it had been evident that comedy would be an important part of programming, no one, in the primitive and experimental days of 1946, could have foreseen the course it would take.

Most comedians came to the home screens after years of basic training in vaudeville, burlesque, the theater, or radio. And most were unprepared to meet television's peculiar and exacting demands. In burlesque or vaudeville a comedy act could be constructed and developed before live audiences in a thousand little theaters in the hinterlands; by the time a comedian became a top banana, his material had been burnished to a high gloss through years of trial and error. Television changed all that. The training grounds vanished; preparation time was telescoped from years into hours; and every appearance before the cameras was like opening at The Palace.

This posed a cruel dilemma for comedians. To maintain their stature (and market value), television exposure was a necessity, yet the medium's voracious appetite for fresh material and creative technique was simply beyond the capacity of most of the funnymen. In time, though often with great reluctance, most of them took a crack at it. One by one the giants of American comedy trooped to the stage to face the unblinking red eye, some for a few hours of guest appearances, others for a season or two with their own shows. Nearly all such attempts were abortive. As a

CHAPTER I

group, the comedians fell victim to the technological revolution in show business.

There were exceptions: Berle and Caesar and Skelton attacked the medium head on and shaped it to their own advantage; Benny and Hope made the transition by adding a visual dimension to an established radio format. But for most of the comedians television was an artificial environment, unlike any other in their experience. Though in many cases they were enormously talented performers, they could not successfully adapt to the new surroundings for any sustained period. Many found themselves relying heavily on directors, producers, and a horde of gag writers, but these efforts tended to dilute rather than enhance their comedy image, and they were quickly dismissed by a jaded and insatiable audience.

The high mortality rate among comedians forced television to reevaluate the concept of comedy as it related to the picture tube. Tradition was cast aside and what emerged were personalities, performers who, like Willy Loman, wanted only to be liked. Along with them came the situation comedies, which emphasized home, love, and family, and rarely contained more than a few legitimate chuckles. The quest was for warmth, not laughter.

Although it would still have room for an occasional attempt at something new or unusual in comedy (Jonathan Winters or *TW3*), by the mid-sixties television had relegated the comedian to guest shots on variety shows, exile in Las Vegas, or a forced retirement in which he damned the Nielsen ratings as he muttered over his scrapbooks. A bland curtain had descended, and the laughter had become muted and almost inaudible.

Berle's version of a vacationing Englishman, in a sketch with comedienne Gracie Fields.

MILTON BERLE
was known as "Mr. Television," and with some justice. His show *The Texaco Star Theater* went on the air in 1948 and remained on (with some changes in title and sponsorship) until 1956. Tuesday night was Berle Night, and in those early days owners of television receivers could usually expect half the neighborhood to drop in for a Tuesday-night visit. Another typical scene of that era was the crowd gathered on the sidewalk outside an appliance store, watching Uncle Miltie through the plate-glass window. Berle was a major factor in establishing the popularity of the new medium, and he was undoubtedly responsible for the purchase of the first television set in many households. His shows featured brash and raucous comedy, guest stars, and lavish production. In later seasons, Berle appeared as the host of another comedy series, as a guest on both variety and dramatic programs, and, briefly, as the comedy emcee of a bowling show.

With guest Bob Smith, Berle appears in a typically outlandish costume.

Ruth Gilbert played Berle's secretary, Max.

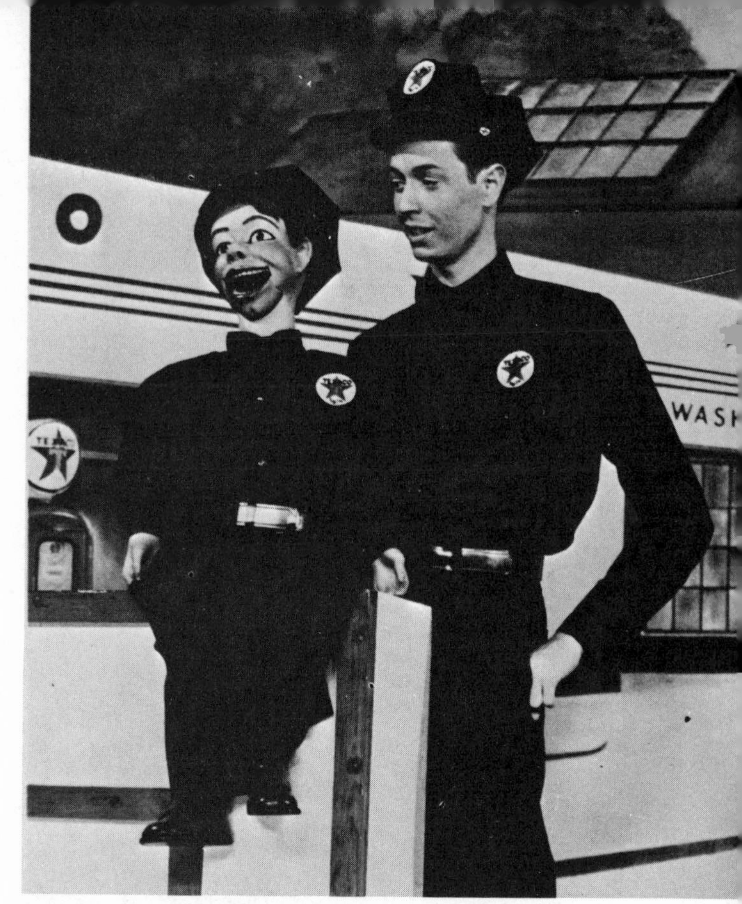

Ventriloquist Jimmy Nelson and his dummy, Danny O'Day, were permanent cast members.

Pitchman Sid Stone, whose "I'll tell you what I'm gonna do" became a conversational fad.

A typical rehearsal scene. Berle was noted for his long hours of rehearsal and his meticulous attention to every detail of his programs.

JACKIE GLEASON
has long been a performer in the theater, nightclubs, and motion pictures, but his greatest popularity and his most creative comedy efforts resulted from his work in television. With a few brief hiatuses, he has appeared regularly since 1950. In that time, he has introduced a gallery of comedy characters, each a sharply etched portrait with depth and dimension. In recent years he has made a number of dramatic appearances, most notably as Minnesota Fats in the film "The Hustler."

Gleason, costarring with Rosemary DeCamp, was the first Chester Riley in *The Life of Riley* series (1950). William Bendix later took over the role.

On *Cavalcade of Stars,* Gleason introduced "The Honeymooners," a series of sketches featuring Pert Kelton as his wife.

Reginald Van Gleason III.

Charley the Loudmouth, with Art Carney.

Joe the Bartender.

The Poor Soul.

SID CAESAR first appeared on the *Admiral Broadway Revue* in 1949. The program was later entitled *Your Show of Shows* and remained on the air until the summer of 1954. Featured on the ninety-minute productions were Imogene Coca, Carl Reiner, Howard Morris, Marguerite Piazza, the Hamilton Trio, the Billy Williams Quartet, and the dance team of Bambi Linn and Rod Alexander. From the outset it was clear that Caesar possessed a comedy talent of extraordinary range, and the show constantly reflected his versatility. Ably abetted by Coca, Reiner, and Morris, he presented pantomimes, sketches, and, most memorably, savagely satirical burlesques of motion pictures and operas. When *Your Show of Shows* ended, Caesar and Coca went their separate ways. They were later reunited as a team for a single season, 1958. Caesar has since starred on Broadway in "Little Me" and has appeared as a guest star on numerous shows.

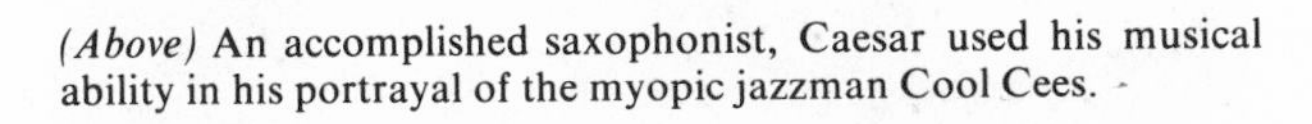

(Above) An accomplished saxophonist, Caesar used his musical ability in his portrayal of the myopic jazzman Cool Cees.

(Top, right) In a takeoff on the musical tastes of the day, Carl Reiner and Howard Morris join Caesar in a trio called The Haircuts.

(Right) In one of his most famous lampoons, Caesar became author and storyteller Somerset Winterset.

(Bottom, right) Art Carney is the director, as silent-film star Caesar enjoys his daily milk bath.

(Below) One of the Caesar-Coca trademarks was the ability to perform a sketch realistically on a bare stage, with no elaborate props or costumes.

In the course of his many shows, four stars appeared as Caesar's "wives." They were *(Right)* Imogene Coca, *(Above)* Nanette Fabray, *(Top, right)* Janet Blair, and *(Below)* Gisele MacKenzie.

(Below) In this movie satire Audrey Meadows watches intently as Caesar, a man of simple tastes, eats a meal consisting only of boiled bread. □ *(Bottom, left)* Eating scenes abounded in the Caesar shows. Here Cliff Norton looks on as Caesar, Carl Reiner, and Howard Morris attack a Chinese dinner. (During another memorable meal, the boys were served a flaming Cherries Jubilee. The flame, of course, refused to go out.)

Red Skelton
first appeared on television in 1953, and *The Red Skelton Show* has been a fixture ever since. Over the years, Skelton has developed dozens of character vignettes, each a small gem of buffoonery. Although best known for his broad, physical comedy, Skelton often injects a note of pathos in his portrayals. In the classifications generally assigned to his trade, Skelton is considered a clown rather than a comic or comedian; as such, his fellow professionals usually rate him the master. Audiences, as interpreted by Nielsen, also award him top ratings.

With Vincent Price and Chanin Hale, Skelton appears as the scourge of the badmen, Sheriff Deadeye.

Janis Paige plays Hatti Mari, a glamorous spy, in this fantasy sketch featuring the befuddled Clem Kaddiddlehopper.

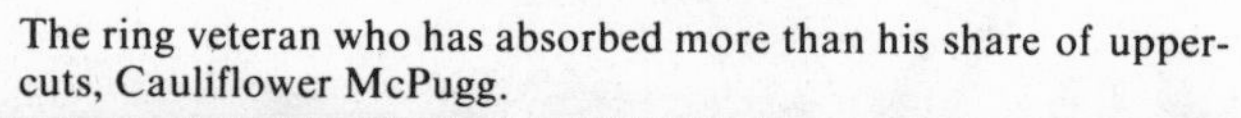

The ring veteran who has absorbed more than his share of upper-cuts, Cauliflower McPugg.

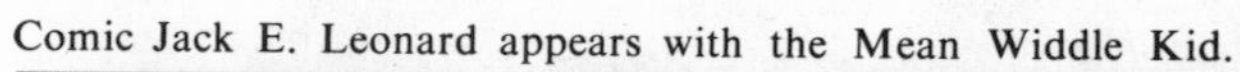

Comic Jack E. Leonard appears with the Mean Widdle Kid.

(Top, left) Skelton as a Japanese soldier in this scene with guest Sessue Hayakawa.

(Bottom, left) In a musical sketch with Helen Traubel.

(Below) Still in costume as a braggart politician, Skelton takes a curtain call.

Bob Hope
cannot be ranked competitively with other show-business personalities; he stands alone as an American institution. *The Bob Hope Show* first appeared on a regular basis in 1952, although Hope had starred in a number of programs for some three years before that date. For the most part his television work has been confined to monthly specials; notable among these have been the Christmas shows for servicemen in remote areas. Hope's popularity and acceptance are such that whoops of laughter greet his barbed comments on social and political problems, comments that might, in other hands, be considered a breach of taste or manners. The basic format of Hope's comedy shows—a monologue followed by sketches with guest stars—has remained unchanged since his radio days in the thirties, but the passing years have diminished neither the polish nor the exuberance of his performance.

(Top) In an early series called *Star Spangled Revue,* Hope appears with guest Frank Sinatra.

(Above) Always known as an admirer of feminine charm, Hope appeared with Jane Russell in the premiere program of his 1954 season.

(Left) With guest star Beatrice Lillie.

(Above) Hope is perhaps best known, and certainly most loved, for the hundreds of shows performed for servicemen since World War II. Here he introduces a member of one of his troupes, actress Marie McDonald.

(Above) Hope (shown here with Oscar-presenter Lana Turner) has been the perennial emcee of the Academy Awards telecasts. While the show itself frequently takes a critical pasting, Hope's contribution is usually outstanding.

(Below) With guests Natalie Wood and the Crosby Brothers (Gary, Dennis, Philip, and Lindsay), Hope has the role of Scarface in this gangster sketch.

KEN MURRAY
first presented his show in 1950 and remained on the air for three seasons. Murray was a veteran showman with an extensive background in vaudeville and the theater, and he made the transition to television easily. His shows were a mélange of music, comedy, drama, and novelty acts. More recently Murray has turned a hobby into a profitable vocation: he has made frequent television appearances with his collection of old home movies featuring famous personalities of the entertainment world.

(Right) He was both star and producer of *The Ken Murray Show*, which was billed as a "variety extravaganza."

(Below) With Laurie Anders, who was best known for saying "Ah love the waaaahd open spaces."

(Above) Benny's daughter Joan, along with his wife Mary Livingstone, appeared with Jack in this 1954 program.

(Top, left) Eddie "Rochester" Anderson, whose gravel voice has delighted Benny audiences for some thirty years.

(Left) Benny conducts the Twist with Hugh Downs, Rock Hudson, and Dennis Day.

(Bottom, left) The musical aggregation in this 1954 program included Fred MacMurray, Tony Martin, Dick Powell, Kirk Douglas, and Dan Dailey.

(Below) With Marilyn Monroe, who made her television debut on Benny's show in 1953.

JACK BENNY
was first seen on television in a regular series in 1952. He brought with him the family of players long familiar to radio audiences: Don Wilson, Dennis Day, Rochester, Mary Livingstone, and Mel Blanc. Benny's radio trademarks—the long, pregnant pause and the exasperated "Well!"—were bolstered by some visual affectations: the prancing walk, the hand held to the cheek, and the look of numbed horror as he was beset by life's little tragedies. Visible too were the celebrated Maxwell, the underground bank vault, and the long-abused violin. Benny's low-pitched, underplayed situation comedy proved as attractive in television as it had in radio. His work today is largely confined to specials and infrequent guest appearances.

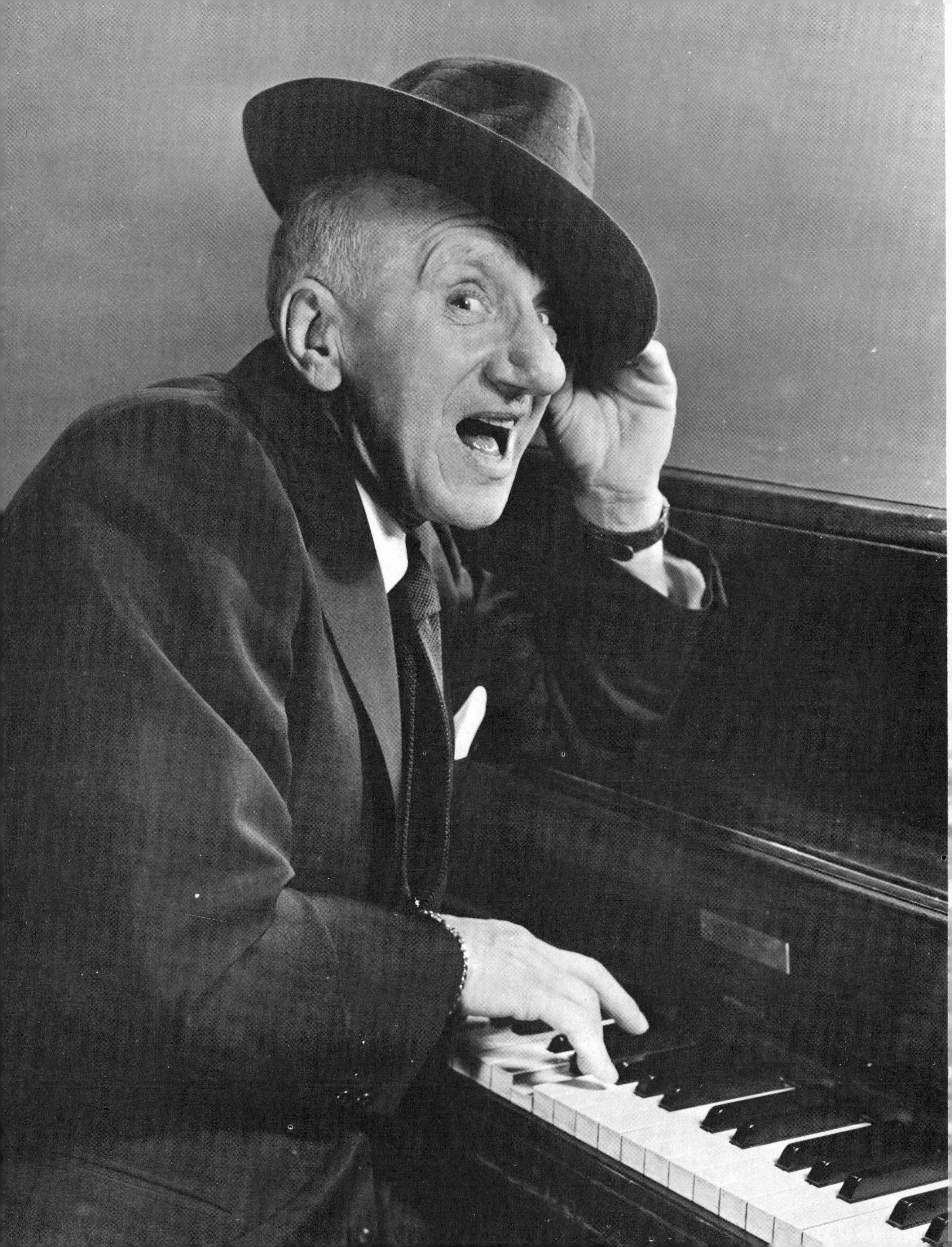

Jimmy Durante

was seen frequently on television in the early fifties on such shows as *The Colgate Comedy Hour, All Star Revue,* and *Four Star Revue.* His previous work in nightclubs, radio, vaudeville, and the theater served him well, and viewers were soon entranced by the little man with the beady eyes, the formidable schnoz, and the tortured vocabulary. In addition to his singing, dancing, and keyboard clowning, Durante's special stamp is the trace of wistful melancholy in his character. On television this was highlighted in several ways. There was the slow exit, coat slung over his shoulder, amid the beams of overhead spots. There was the inevitable good-night to Mrs. Calabash (whom Jimmy has recently identified as his first wife). More recently there was the Durante rendition—sans comedy—of "September Song." In 1954–56, Durante starred in his own series, *The Texaco Star Theater.* Now, however, he makes only occasional appearances on television.

Eddie Jackson and Durante are the surviving members of the famed vaudeville team of Clayton, Jackson, and Durante.

The suave Durante greets guest star Ethel Barrymore.

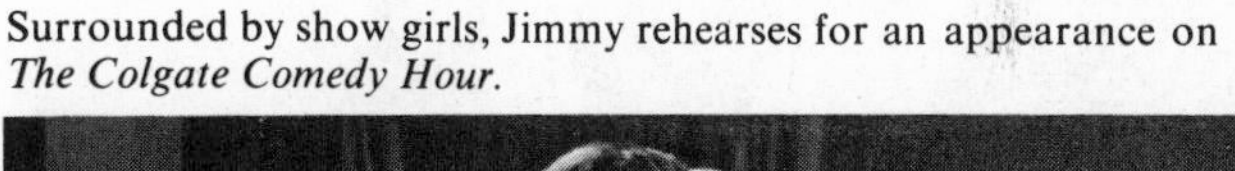

Surrounded by show girls, Jimmy rehearses for an appearance on *The Colgate Comedy Hour.*

DEAN MARTIN AND JERRY LEWIS made their television debut on Ed Sullivan's first *Toast of the Town* in June, 1948. From that point on, they made numerous guest appearances before appearing for six seasons, on a rotating basis, on *The Colgate Comedy Hour*. They were, in many respects, the perfect comedy team. Martin's good looks and smooth baritone balanced Lewis' impishness and frantic comedy. The team split in 1956, at a time when their popularity and earning power had reached dizzying heights. Despite some predictions to the contrary, each became enormously successful on his own. Lewis wrote, directed, and starred in a long string of motion pictures which, without exception, have been box-office bonanzas. Lewis has confined most of his television work to guest shots and specials (including telethons for victims of muscular dystrophy). In 1963 he embarked on an expensive and much-heralded Saturday-night series which ended quickly after being universally pronounced a disaster. Martin, too, turned to motion pictures, and is now considered to be a stellar box-office attraction. He got his own television series in 1965.

(Top) In a typical scene, Martin appears pained as Lewis demonstrates his vocal abilities. □ *(Above)* In their early days, at least, the team enjoyed themselves immensely as they worked. □ *(Left)* The adjectives most often used to describe Martin and Lewis were "wild," "zany," and "uninhibited." All were accurate. □ *(Below)* Rehearsing for *The Colgate Comedy Hour*, Martin attempts a song as Lewis leads the musicians astray.

(Left) You Bet Your Life: The one and only Groucho Marx was the star of this comedy quiz which was more comedy than quiz. First seen in 1950, it featured a secret word, a stuffed duck, some wacky contestants, and endless quips by the master.

(Below) It Pays to Be Ignorant: This panel played it for laughs, too: (left to right) Harry McNaughton, Lulu McConnell, George Shelton, and Tom Howard. The video version arrived in 1949.

(Bottom) Pantomime Quiz: One of television's perennials since the late forties, this show was usually a summer replacement, but occasionally got a spot on fall schedules. The charade players on this series got their quota of laughs, but always played the game with ferocious intensity. In the 1951 photo shown, they are (left to right) Jackie Coogan, Vincent Price, host Mike Stokey, and Hans Conried.

(Top, left) MAKE ME LAUGH: In this 1958 effort professional comics tried to extract smiles from one another within a brief time limit. The three here are (left to right) Sid Gould, Harvey Stone, and Henny Youngman.

(Top, right) THE GREAT TALENT HUNT: Arnold Stang (left) assisted Henry Morgan in introducing contestants who displayed what might charitably be called eccentric talents.

(Above) LAUGH LINE: The panelists had to supply punch lines on this 1959 show. Dick Van Dyke was the emcee, and the panel included (left to right) Elaine May, Mike Nichols, Dorothy Loudon, and Orson Bean.

(Left) KEEP TALKING: The object of this 1958 game was to start a story that your opponent had to finish. Here Joey Bishop embarks on a flight of rhetoric as Danny Dayton waits his turn.

(Left) CELEBRITY TIME: Actor Conrad Nagel was the host of this 1949 fun-and-games session. Regular panelists included Kyle McDonnell and Yale football coach Herman Hickman.

(Below) TWO FOR THE MONEY: This 1953 quiz show had Herb Shriner as emcee and (far left) Dr. Mason Gross of Rutgers University as a kind of referee.

(Bottom) JUDGE FOR YOURSELF: Fred Allen made many television appearances, including a one-year stint, beginning in 1953, as host of this show. But he was never to recapture the glories of his radio days. One of his finest video contributions was the narration of "The Jazz Age" on *Project 20;* ironically, the program was telecast some nine months after his death, in 1956. He is shown here with a vocal group, The Skylarks.

CAPTAIN KANGAROO:
Bob Keeshan donned a uniform cap and a walrus mustache in 1955 when he became the Captain, and thus began a long reign as the dominant figure in preschool children's programming. Until that time most children's shows, with a few notable exceptions, had been loud, gaudy, and rather limited in creative imagination. (Keeshan himself had once served as Clarabell on the *Howdy Doody Show.*) *Captain Kangaroo* was an abrupt departure from the past. Its emphasis was on quiet conversation, gentle fantasy, and easy-to-swallow morsels of an educational nature. The program's acceptance and popularity seemed to grow with each passing year, as did the number of awards and citations from groups of parents, teachers, and educators.

Howdy Doody

was first telecast in 1947 and remained on the air until 1960. The show was a loud and lively entertainment effort, and although it made no pretense of being anything else, parents sometimes complained that the program had no redeeming educational value. Buffalo Bob Smith was the creator and host of the show, assisted by a succession of clowns named Clarabell. Since children who attended the telecasts often appeared on camera, the demand for tickets was overwhelming, and the waiting list a long one. At one time, it was said, expectant mothers would write to request tickets for their unborn children.

(Left) The original Howdy Doody as the audience saw him in the first six weeks of the television show, before his contours were changed.

(Below) With youngsters in the "peanut gallery" behind them, Bob Smith, Howdy, and Clarabell celebrate the show's tenth anniversary.

SOUPY SALES:
He started with a local show in Detroit *(Soupy's On),* graduated to a network program, and finally landed in New York, where he launched a daily local show that was syndicated widely. Soupy's specialties are the pie in the face (at least one a show, sometimes dozens); outrageous riddles, puns, and old jokes; and conversations with his animal friends (here, he is caressed by Black Tooth, "the kindest dog in the country"). He has always been a favorite of the youngsters, but recently he has also become "in" with the hipster set.

(Above) The late Leon Errol performs his famous drunk act on *The Ed Wynn Show* in 1950. The two had appeared together in "The Ziegfeld Follies of 1914."

ED WYNN,
known to several generations of Americans as "The Fire Chief" and "The Perfect Fool," arrived on television with *The Ed Wynn Show* in 1949. The show ran for two years, after which Wynn appeared in several other comedy-revue series. His bizarre costumes and high-pitched cackle were absent from television after 1952, until his dramatic (in more ways than one) reappearance in 1956. In that year Wynn essayed a serious role in the *Playhouse 90* blockbuster "Requiem for a Heavyweight." After decades as a comedy performer, he astonished both critics and audience with his skillful adjustment to serious drama. His success paved the way to a new phase of his career; he was subsequently featured as a dramatic actor in many television shows and motion pictures. In 1958 he did a situation-comedy series.

(Above) ABBOTT AND COSTELLO: Seen here doing their famed "Who's on First?" routine, the team made many appearances on *The Colgate Comedy Hour* and other variety programs.

(Below) TALLULAH BANKHEAD: After her success in radio's "The Big Show," she became hostess of *All Star Revue* on television.

(Top) RAY BOLGER: A guest performer on comedy and variety shows, Bolger has also starred in his own series *(Washington Square* and *Where's Raymond?).* □ *(Above)* CLIFF NORTON: Besides stints with *Garroway at Large* and *Your Show of Shows,* Norton appeared in the syndicated *Public Life of Cliff Norton* and *Funny Manns.* □ *(Below)* JUDY CANOVA: In the fifties, the singer-comedienne was a frequent guest artist.

EDDIE CANTOR,
after a long and illustrious career in almost every phase of show business, came to television via *The Colgate Comedy Hour* in 1950. He was with the show for four seasons. Ill health forced him to curtail his activities thereafter, but he undertook several comedy and dramatic guest appearances during the next several years. He was the host and occasional star of a syndicated series, *The Eddie Cantor Comedy Theater,* prior to his death in 1964.

(Top, left) As "Maxie the Taxi," a character created on *The Colgate Comedy Hour.*

(Bottom, left) With guest star Dorothy Lamour.

(Below) The banjo eyes and outstretched hands were Cantor's identification.

SAM LEVENSON: A master storyteller, Levenson starred in his own shows in 1950 and 1951, then became a game-show panelist and guest performer. He is seen here with his son, in 1952.

JOE E. BROWN: He was the star of *The Buick Circus Hour* in 1952.

AL PEARCE: In 1950 Pearce brought to television the character he had made famous in radio: Elmer Blurt, the low-pressure salesman.

JACK CARTER: Shown here with singer Donald Richards and show girls Jackie Lockridge and Susan Stewart, Carter starred in *The Saturday Night Revue* in 1950 and 1951.

MARTHA RAYE
brought her high-decibel comedy to television in 1951 on *All Star Revue*. After two seasons, she starred in *The Martha Raye Show,* which was on the air for four years. She has been a guest star on almost every comedy and variety show of note, and was a frequent visitor to *The Steve Allen Show*.

(Left) As a torchy siren, Martha unleashes a come-hither look.

(Bottom, left) In a typical slapstick sketch, she entertains a gentleman caller (Cesar Romero).

(Below) When his ring career ended, Rocky Graziano found a new kind of fame as Martha Raye's comedy foil. They are shown here on *All Star Revue* in 1953.

JOEY ADAMS: Shown here with double-talk king Al Kelly on a 1953 quiz show called *Back That Fact,* Adams was also a comedy performer on other early variety shows.

JACKIE KANNON: He made a number of visits to Hoagy Carmichael's *Saturday Night Revue.*

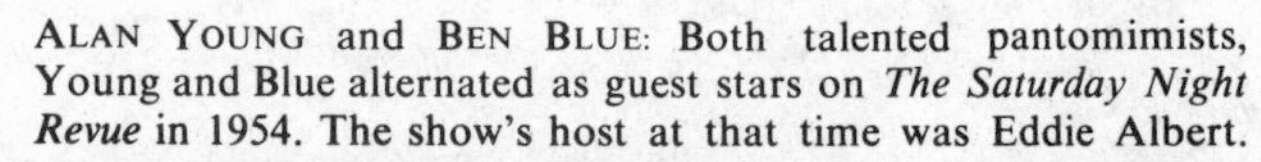

ALAN YOUNG and BEN BLUE: Both talented pantomimists, Young and Blue alternated as guest stars on *The Saturday Night Revue* in 1954. The show's host at that time was Eddie Albert.

DONALD O'CONNOR: With sidekick Sid Miller (at the piano), singer-dancer-comedian O'Connor made many appearances on *The Colgate Comedy Hour.*

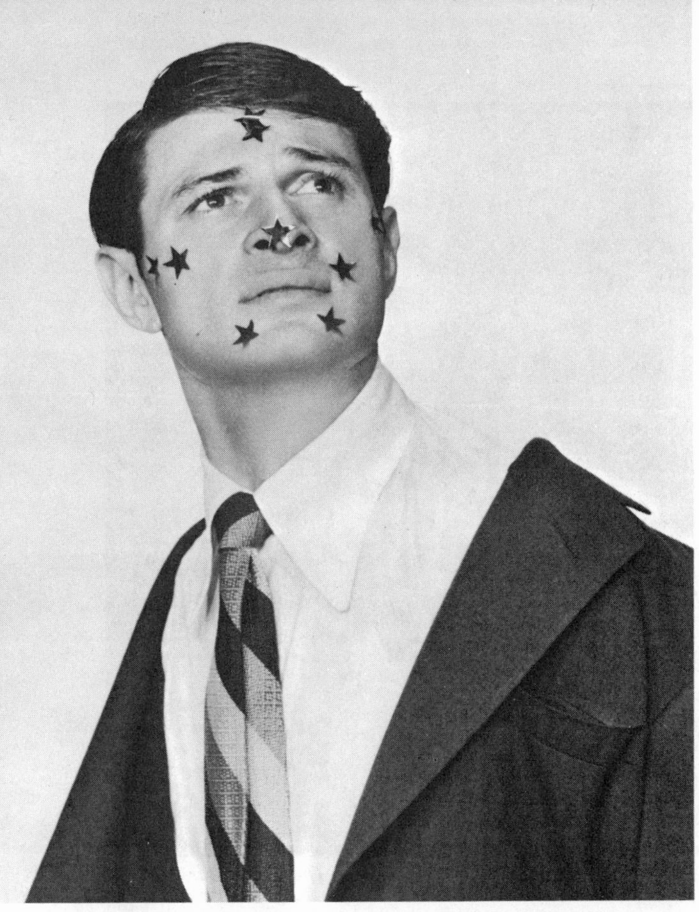

LARRY STORCH: A featured performer on *Cavalcade of Stars* (which he publicized with this photograph), he later starred in *The Larry Storch Show* (1953) and *F Troop* (beginning in 1965).

PHIL SILVERS: Shown here with comic Joey Faye and the chorus girls from *Showtime . . . U.S.A.* (in 1951), Silvers was seen as a guest performer numerous times prior to the introduction of his Sergeant Bilko series.

GENE SHELDON: The comedian and instrumentalist made many appearances on *The Colgate Comedy Hour*.

THE RITZ BROTHERS: The knockabout trio worked occasionally on television, but preferred to confine their activities mostly to nightclubs.

(Above) JACK HALEY: He was emcee of *The Four Star Revue* in 1951.

(Top, left) GEORGE JESSEL: With his guest, Fred Allen, on *All Star Revue* in 1953. In recent years Jessel has made numerous guest appearances on *The Tonight Show* and *The Jackie Gleason Show.*

(Left) BOB AND RAY: Bob Elliott and Ray Goulding (with cast member Audrey Meadows) on *The Bob and Ray Show* in 1953.

(Bottom, left) JACK CARSON: Shown here in a sketch from *The Four Star Revue,* Carson later turned to dramatic roles.

(Below) OLSEN AND JOHNSON: In 1949 they starred in their own show, *Fireball Fun for All.*

PINKY LEE,
an ex-burlesque comic, made his television debut on *Those Two* in 1951. For a time it was fashionable for other comedians to poke fun at Lee, but *Those Two* remained on the air for three years, and Lee's children's show was similarly successful.

(Above) A capable dancer and storyteller, Lee used both talents to advantage on his children's program, *The Pinky Lee Show.*

(Right) With costar Martha Stewart on *Those Two,* a variety series. Miss Stewart was succeeded by Vivian Blaine.

HENNY AND ROCKY: Henny Youngman, Rocky Graziano, and singer Marion Colby teamed up for *The Henny and Rocky Show,* a program designed to fill the gap between the end of the Wednesday-night fights and the next program on the schedule.

WAYNE AND SHUSTER: Originally booked as an act on *The Ed Sullivan Show,* this team of Canadian comics made numerous guest appearances and later starred in their own situation-comedy series.

DOODLES WEAVER: One of television's pioneer performers (he appeared regularly in 1946), Weaver later starred on his own series, *The Doodles Weaver Show.*

DAVE KING: An English comedian and singer, King was a summer replacement for *The Perry Como Show.*

RED BUTTONS,

a former burlesque and Catskill-resorts comedian, burst into television in 1952. His show was an instantaneous hit. But after its first season *The Red Buttons Show* floundered, and despite some tinkering with the format it disappeared from view in 1954. Buttons' difficulties with writers were legendary, and there is no accurate tally of the total number who were employed by the show at one time or another. A trade joke of the time had a writer wandering into Madison Square Garden and, confronted by a screaming mob of some 18,000 fans, retreating in panic because he thought he had stumbled into a meeting of Buttons' writers. Buttons went to Hollywood, and was voted an Academy Award for his appearance in the film "Sayonara." He returned to television in 1966 with a spy-spoof series, *The Double Life of Henry Phyfe*.

(Top, left) In his nostalgic little-boy role, the Kupke Kid.

(Above) As a punch-drunk fighter, Rocky Buttons.

(Right) The cupped ear and "The Ho-Ho Song" were Buttons' trademarks.

(Below) With Phyllis Kirk, who played his wife after the show had become a situation comedy.

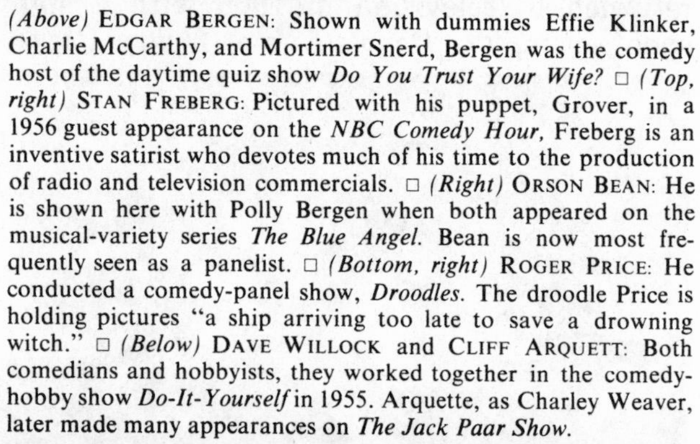

(Above) EDGAR BERGEN: Shown with dummies Effie Klinker, Charlie McCarthy, and Mortimer Snerd, Bergen was the comedy host of the daytime quiz show *Do You Trust Your Wife?* □ *(Top, right)* STAN FREBERG: Pictured with his puppet, Grover, in a 1956 guest appearance on the *NBC Comedy Hour,* Freberg is an inventive satirist who devotes much of his time to the production of radio and television commercials. □ *(Right)* ORSON BEAN: He is shown here with Polly Bergen when both appeared on the musical-variety series *The Blue Angel.* Bean is now most frequently seen as a panelist. □ *(Bottom, right)* ROGER PRICE: He conducted a comedy-panel show, *Droodles.* The droodle Price is holding pictures "a ship arriving too late to save a drowning witch." □ *(Below)* DAVE WILLOCK and CLIFF ARQUETT: Both comedians and hobbyists, they worked together in the comedy-hobby show *Do-It-Yourself* in 1955. Arquette, as Charley Weaver, later made many appearances on *The Jack Paar Show.*

ERNIE KOVACS
made his first national appearances on television in 1951 and 1952 in several series that originated in Philadelphia. He was the possessor of a wildly original comic mind, and he employed a casual, low-key technique in his comedy. He was especially creative in his use of cameras and technical equipment, with the result that most of his shows abounded in visual trickery. *The Ernie Kovacs Show* was on the air in 1955 and 1956, after which Kovacs starred in a number of specials and appeared as a comedy guest on other shows. His brilliant career was ended by his death, in an automobile accident, in 1962.

(Above) With his wife, singer Edie Adams, in an outer-space sketch on *The Ernie Kovacs Show* in 1956. □ *(Left)* Flourishing his ever-present cigar in the 1960 show *Take a Good Look*. □ *(Below)* As the lisping, half-soused poet, Percy Dovetonsils.

GEORGE GOBEL,
an easygoing, guitar-strumming comedian, had made several television appearances in the early fifties before his debut on *The George Gobel Show* in 1954. The cast included Jeff Donnell and singer Peggy King. The program enjoyed great popularity, and before long the country was awash with Gobelisms, the most prominent of which was "Well, I'll be a dirty bird." Along with guest appearances and nightclub work, Gobel currently performs in television commercials.

(Above) With Jeff Donnell, who appeared as his wife Alice. In 1959 the role was played by Phyllis Avery.

(Top, left) In 1957 Gobel and Eddie Fisher alternated each week as host and guest star of their program.

(Bottom, left) Gobel as a mad scientist, with singer Anita Bryant.

(Below) As a reluctant cowpoke, with Kirk Douglas.

ALLEN SHERMAN: A former television producer *(I've Got a Secret, The Steve Allen Show)*, Sherman's highly successful song parodies ("My Son, the Folk Singer") have made him a much-sought-after television performer.

JONATHAN WINTERS: After more than a decade as a guest on everybody's show (and a brief stint with his own fifteen-minute show), he starred in a series of specials in 1964. More recently he has appeared in several motion pictures.

BOB NEWHART: Newhart's unique style and delivery first brought him success via comedy phonograph albums; he later starred on *The Bob Newhart Show* and *The Entertainers*.

ALAN KING: A skilled monologist, King is most frequently seen on *The Ed Sullivan Show* and *The Tonight Show*.

DANNY KAYE

was yet another product of the Catskill Mountains resorts. After a dazzling performance in the Broadway hit "Lady in the Dark," he embarked on a successful career that included radio, motion pictures, and one-man concert appearances. For many years he resisted the blandishments of television, and only in 1963 did he undertake the rigors of a regular series. Although his early acclaim derived from his ability to handle the tongue-twisting lyrics of special material (mostly written by his wife Sylvia Fine), he has now largely abandoned the "git-gat-gittle" songs and has become one of the most versatile entertainers of our day. Kaye possesses a superb ear for language and inflection (as in his classic impression of Sir Harry Lauder), is a nimble dancer and better-than-adequate singer, and owns the most expressive hands in show business.

(Top, right) In 1957, Kaye appeared in a *See It Now* program entitled "The Secret World of Danny Kaye." In it the comedian visited with children all over the world to demonstrate the work being done by UNICEF. The show had great emotional impact, and was ample proof that true artistry could overcome the problems posed by language and geographical barriers. □ *(Right)* In a special ("An Hour with Danny Kaye") which appeared on the air prior to Kaye's regular series, the comedian heckles trumpeter Louis Armstrong. □ *(Below)* With guest star Lucille Ball in a production number (choreographed by Tony Charmoli) on *The Danny Kaye Show.*

THAT WAS THE WEEK THAT WAS originated in England and quickly became famed for its mocking irreverence and savage lampoons of people and events in the news. The show's American counterpart, however, wavered erratically between sophisticated satire and broad comedy with mass appeal. As a result, it never developed a large audience devoted to either brand of humor. But, despite its shortcomings, *TW3* represented an innovation in American television, for it often displayed a courage and daring previously lacking on our home screens. The program was occasionally accused of political partisanship, though it made obvious attempts to balance its books by bludgeoning both political parties. Despite its flaws, many critics saw in *TW3* a glimmering of hope for the future; though the show itself might perish, a precedent had been set for similar excursions in satire. But when *TW3* expired, it left no heirs, and television comedy continued in the patterns and formats familiar to viewers since 1946.

(Above) David Frost, who had appeared on the British version of the show, was a frequent performer over here too.

(Top, left) The female stars of *TW3* were (left to right) Nancy Ames, Phyllis Newman, and Pat Englund.

(Left) Nancy Ames, "The TW3 Girl," introduced each show with a musical commentary on the happenings of the preceding week.

Personalities Plus

MANY OF TELEVISION'S GREATS had already achieved celebrity or stardom in other branches of the entertainment business before they tackled television, but one very special group can be considered only as the progeny of the picture tube. For lack of a more descriptive name, they have become known as "television personalities." Their unique talent is the ability to succeed without benefit of a unique talent, at least in the traditional sense. In terms of television, however, they possess a formidable talent, desirable above all others. They can reach out and grab an audience. They establish rapport; they blend.

The stars can sing, dance, or play the marimba. The personalities, almost to a man, would have been the also-rans on Ted Mack's *Amateur Hour* (including, of course, Ted Mack himself). But the personalities can generate from the audience feelings of love, affection, or mere tolerance (often this is sufficient), and the record clearly indicates that this accomplishment almost guarantees a long and lucrative television life. Such a consummation is devoutly to be wished, even by the world's greatest marimba player.

Personalities are usually called hosts or hostesses, a most apt description. Like the hosts of a well-planned cocktail party, they contribute to the occasion by circulating quietly through the proceedings, never intruding unnecessarily, always attempting a

CHAPTER II

smooth intermingling of their more volatile guests. They beam and greet their guests on arrival; they chat briefly and engagingly, perhaps including a mild jest or two; they have a smile and a handshake when the guests depart. Al Jolson might not have approved, but Perle Mesta would.

Because their careers depend on it, personalities are careful not to upset the delicate equilibrium which has brought them viewer love or viewer sufferance. They are, generally speaking, status-quo people who shy away from controversy or radical innovation lest they antagonize any considerable segment of the audience. Thus their public image is fuzzy and ill-defined; sharper definition might trigger sharper reaction, and personalities understand that television longevity frequently depends not on reaction, but on the lack of it. (Jack Paar is a notable exception to all of this. His mercurial temperament and devastating candor were essential ingredients of his charm, and audience acceptance of his outbursts is worth pondering. He was either a pioneer, blazing new trails for the personalities, or he was television's first safety valve.) It should be made clear, however, that detachment is not necessarily a self-imposed condition, but rather one that is considered a requirement of the medium. Perhaps it is true that the mass audience demands that the personality be homogenized, but it is also true that everyone bought black automobiles until other colors became available. Until television decides that other colors are marketable, almost every personality will continue to conceal emotion and intellect behind the sunshine of his smile.

Topo Gigio, the Italian mouse, has been a longtime favorite on the show. Speaking in heavily accented English, the mechanical rodent does comedy routines with Sullivan, who acts as straight man.

ED SULLIVAN
is a television phenomenon. A Broadway columnist with no discernible theatrical talent, he appeared on home screens as emcee of *Toast of the Town* in 1948. He seemed, from the beginning, an unlikely selection for the job. Awkward of movement (for years, viewers would write, "What's wrong with his neck?"), thick of speech, plagued with a dozen nervous mannerisms, he did not appear destined for survival in television's competitive wars. But eighteen years later his show was still flying high in the ratings while most of his competition had disappeared without leaving a trace. Sullivan's popularity and longevity are no accidents. He is a master showman. He has an unerring instinct for selecting performers and acts most likely to pique the interest or stir the enthusiasm of an audience that has long since become jaded and blasé. He also pays top dollar and insists on an exclusivity clause which prevents his guests from appearing on competing programs for a set period of time before and after their appearance on his show. Small wonder, then, that Sullivan has presented almost every luminary in the sports and entertainment worlds, many precisely at that moment when public interest in them was at its peak (as in the case of the Beatles, Ingrid Bergman, and Elvis Presley). Sullivan is a man of considerable personal warmth, and for the most part he ignores the gibes aimed in his direction, but some of his feuds (with Walter Winchell, Jack Paar, Jackie Mason) produced some lively verbal fencing. Fred Allen once said that "Ed Sullivan will be around as long as someone else has talent." But Allen, an old vaudevillian himself, must have known that putting together a consistently fine variety program requires more than a little talent.

In the premiere telecast of *Toast of the Town* on June 20, 1948, the cast (left to right) included singing fireman John Kokoman, pianist Eugene List, comedian Jim Kirkwood, comedian Jerry Lewis, dancer Kathryn Lee, composers Richard Rodgers and Oscar Hammerstein 2nd, Ed Sullivan, singer Dean Martin, fight referee Ruby Goldstein, and comedian Lee Goodman. The dancing girls flanking the cast were the original "Toastettes." This show marked the television debut of Martin and Lewis.

(Above) Sullivan's mannerisms make him an inviting target for mimics, and comic Will Jordan often appeared on the show with his impersonations of Sullivan. □ *(Top, right)* With Julia Meade, who for many seasons was the program's commercial spokeswoman. □ *(Right)* A former sportswriter, Sullivan has long delighted in presenting outstanding athletes to his audience. He is shown here with Howard "Hopalong" Cassady, a 1955 All-American. □ *(Bottom, right)* The gyrations of Elvis Presley were such that Sullivan forbade his cameramen to show the singer from the waist down. Thus America was spared shock and outrage and at the same time the show scored a major publicity coup. □ *(Below)* Sullivan devoted an entire program to the Moiseyev Dancers, a Russian folk troupe. The event proved a masterstroke of showmanship and has come to be considered a television classic.

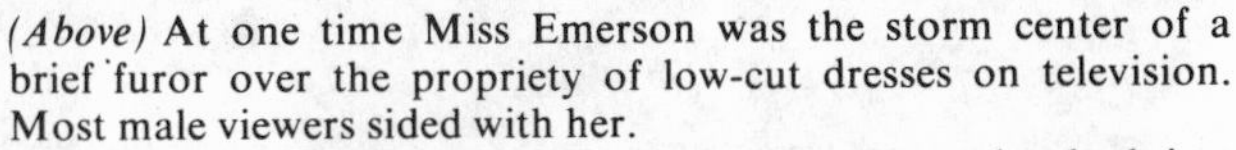

(Above) At one time Miss Emerson was the storm center of a brief furor over the propriety of low-cut dresses on television. Most male viewers sided with her.
(Top, right) With sportswriter Jimmy Cannon, who had just returned from a tour of duty as a war correspondent in Korea.
(Below) With Skitch Henderson (to whom she was married) she interviews the pride of the Brooklyn Dodgers, Jackie Robinson.

FAYE EMERSON
became one of television's most talked-about personalities. After a number of earlier appearances, she bowed with *The Faye Emerson Show* in 1949. The program was broadcast for almost three years, and during that time she made numerous appearances as a guest or panelist on other shows. Since then she has been the hostess of several programs, and for five years she was a panel member of *I've Got a Secret*.

ARTHUR GODFREY
brought to television the same easygoing manner, wry wit, and folksy warmth that had made him one of the great attractions in radio. Television rapidly succumbed to his charms. In 1948 he made his debut with *Talent Scouts,* a show that became a long-running favorite. In 1949 he added *Arthur Godfrey and His Friends,* a variety program. When delivering commercials Godfrey avoided the pompous solemnity that had traditionally surrounded the sponsor's message. As a result, he became the supersalesman of his day and his cheerful disrespect was a highlight of his shows. Godfrey was news, and his troubles with members of his staff and cast were the subject of endless speculation in magazines and newspapers. Similarly, when a plane he piloted was involved in a "buzzing" incident at the Teterboro, New Jersey, airport, the story hit the papers with screaming headlines. In 1959 Godfrey underwent major surgery for cancer. His long battle with the disease and subsequent triumph over it won him renewed respect and admiration.

With his longtime announcer, Tony Marvin.

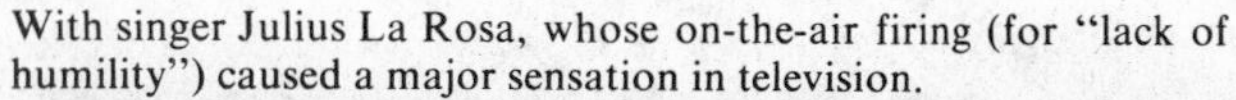

With singer Julius La Rosa, whose on-the-air firing (for "lack of humility") caused a major sensation in television.

(Above) With his trusty ukulele Godfrey accompanies another cast member, Haleloke.

(Top, left) Singers Frank Parker and Marion Marlowe, whose supposed "romance" was long the subject of excited fan gossip.

(Bottom, left) The McGuire Sisters, winners of a 1952 *Talent Scouts* show, became Godfrey regulars in 1953.

(Below) As accompanist for singer Janette Davis.

Arlene Francis
became a *What's My Line?* panelist in 1950 and has remained with the program ever since. In 1952 she presided over *Blind Date,* the television version of a radio show in which she had starred. In 1954 she was the hostess of *Soldier Parade,* and in the same year she became "editor-in-chief" of *Home,* which was described as a women's "service magazine of the air." *Home,* the brainchild of then-NBC president Sylvester "Pat" Weaver, was indeed a programming innovation, both in scope and in maturity of approach. It remained on the air for almost four years but was finally dropped despite the strenuous objections of a loyal audience. An accomplished actress, Miss Francis has also been the proprietress of a radio interview show for some years. She is a woman of infinite poise and charm and is undoubtedly the leading female personality in the entire history of television.

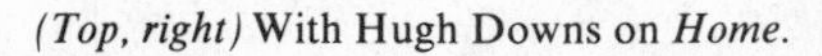

(Top, right) With Hugh Downs on *Home.*

(Bottom, right) As hostess of *Blind Date,* with contestant "Reds" Bagnell, a University of Pennsylvania football star.

(Below) Surrounded by the Fort Dix Soldiers' Chorus on *Soldier Parade.*

Garry Moore

made his television debut in 1950 with a daytime variety show which remained on the air until 1958. Titled *The Garry Moore Show,* it first ran as a daily offering, and in its last four years on a three-times-a-week basis. Moore finally abandoned the show voluntarily, with the words "I'm tired." In 1952 he became moderator of one of Goodson-Todman's most durable properties, *I've Got a Secret,* and did not relinquish this post until 1964. In 1958 he embarked on a new series, as host of a nighttime variety program again titled *The Garry Moore Show.* This program featured a young comedienne, Carol Burnett, and served as her springboard to eventual stardom. Moore took leave of television completely in 1964, then reappeared in a new series in 1966. An ingratiating, relaxed performer, Moore's popularity derives from the sense of friendly rapport he maintains with a family audience.

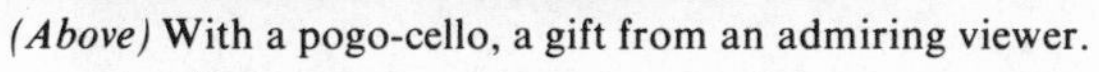

(Above) With a pogo-cello, a gift from an admiring viewer.

(Top, right) In a program finale (left to right): Marion Lorne, Durward Kirby, Mahalia Jackson, Moore, Marge and Gower Champion, Carol Burnett.

(Center, right) Singers Denise Lor and Ken Carson were regulars on the daytime *Garry Moore Show.*

(Right) Moore, Durward Kirby, and guest Gwen Verdon in a sketch on the nighttime *Garry Moore Show* in 1962.

(*Below*) ANITA COLBY: A model and actress dubbed "The Face," she was hostess (in 1954) of *Pepsi-Cola Playhouse*.

(*Above*) VIRGINIA GRAHAM: A veteran radio and television personality, she survived a serious illness and now moderates the provocative chatter show *Girl Talk*.
(*Below*) BETTY FURNESS: A former Powers model, she has had several radio and television shows of her own, but achieved lasting fame as she stood by a refrigerator uttering the immortal words, "You can be sure if it's Westinghouse."

(Above) WENDY BARRIE: *The Wendy Barrie Show* was first broadcast in 1948 and Miss Barrie was among the first performers to become known as television "personalities." She is shown here with guest Juan Carlos Thorez, an Argentine radio and movie star.

(Below) ROBIN CHANDLER: In 1951 she was hostess of *Meet Your Cover Girl* and *Vanity Fair*.

(Above) CARMEL MYERS: A former star of the silent screen (shown here with composer Richard Rodgers, the guest on her premiere show), she was hostess of one of television's early interview programs, *The Carmel Myers Show*.

(Above) ROBERT Q. LEWIS: Shown here as star of a 1950 program called *Robert Q.'s Matinee,* Lewis has since been host, guest, and panelist on dozens of television offerings.

(Below) JAMES MELTON: Known best as a singer, he was also the host (in 1951) of *Ford Festival.* Melton is shown here with tiny Billy Barty, another member of the show's cast.

(Above) RENZO CESANA: He was "The Continental," suave, sophisticated, reeking of manly allure. At his candlelit table for two, his husky voice and perfect manners were supposed to cause female viewers to swoon with ecstasy. Perhaps some did.

(Below) REX MARSHALL: Later to become known as a commercial spokesman ("Hi there, I'm Rex Marshall"), he was host (with actress Sondra Deel) of an early DuMont show, *A Date with Rex.*

(Above) NEIL HAMILTON: Pictured here with guests Rita Gam and Hurd Hatfield, he was host of *Hollywood Screen Test* in 1949.

(Top, left) ROBERT L. RIPLEY: The cartoonist-creator of *Believe It or Not* adapted the series for television after it had become a national byword as a newspaper feature.

(Left) GALEN DRAKE: His show, *This Is Galen Drake*, came to television after he had developed a large and loyal following as a radio performer.

(Bottom, left) JOHN NESBITT: His *Passing Parade* was a perennial favorite as a movie short and then became a television series. He was later host of *Telephone Time*.

(Below) MORTON DOWNEY: The renowned Irish tenor was host of an early interview show, *Star of the Family*. Here he talks with Mrs. Fiorello La Guardia.

ART LINKLETTER
moved from radio to television with his *House Party* in 1952. A glib master of ceremonies, Linkletter kept the mixture of interviews, chatter, and features moving at a brisk pace, and the show rapidly became a daytime favorite with housewives. In 1954 *People Are Funny* made its television debut. It was a show which called upon contestants to perform some unusual stunts, which they always did, surprisingly without protest. While the contents of his shows are usually something less than momentous, Linkletter is especially adept at tying the proceedings together into a bright and cheerful package.

(Top, right) As host of a special, "The Beverly Hills Story," Linkletter chats with Mr. and Mrs. James Stewart.

(Bottom, right) A publicity shot commemorating the start of the second season (1955) of *People Are Funny*.

(Below) On *House Party* Linkletter's interviews with children were a recurring highlight.

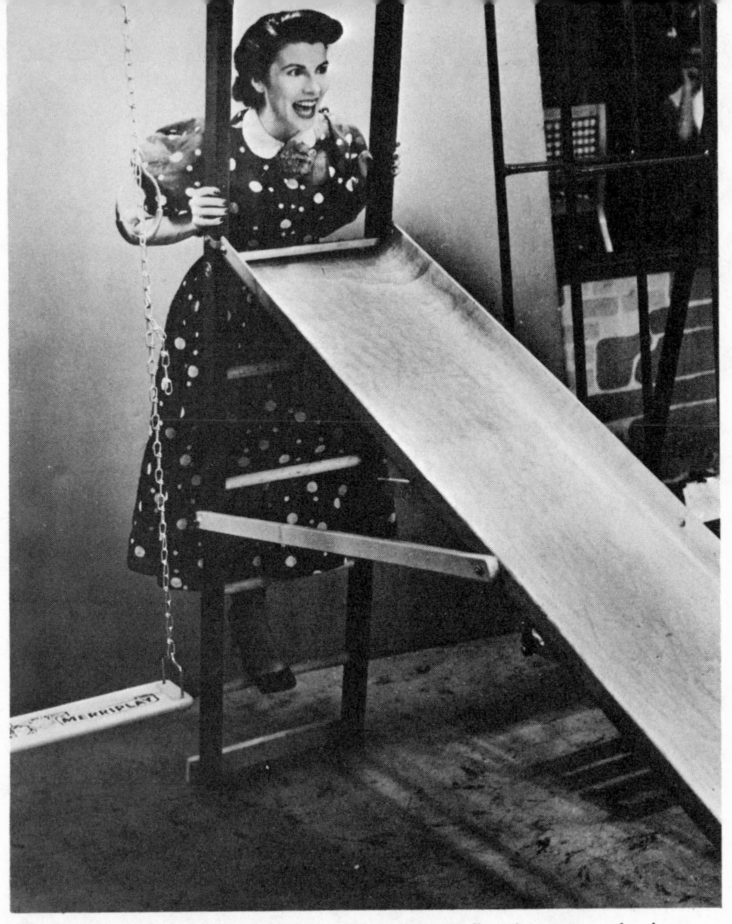

(Above) Kathi Norris: One of television's first hostesses, she is shown here on *The Kathi Norris Show* in 1952.

(Above) Lilli Palmer: *The Lilli Palmer Show* was described as an "informal, at home, personality" program.

(Below) Ilka Chase: In 1950 she was hostess of both *Fashion Magic* and *Glamour-Go-Round.* She was later a panelist on several shows, most notably *Masquerade Party.*

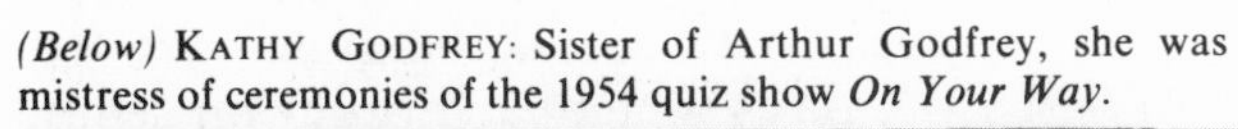

(Below) Kathy Godfrey: Sister of Arthur Godfrey, she was mistress of ceremonies of the 1954 quiz show *On Your Way.*

TED MACK

brought radio's *Original Amateur Hour* to television in 1948. The successor to the late Major Bowes, Mack has maintained the show's format, although the famed gong which announced the untimely end of a disastrous performance has now disappeared. Over the years the general quality of the performers seems to have improved. Gone are the days when each program seemed to have at least one contestant prepared to render "Sweet Adeline" on a bicycle pump. Mack, a gentle, patient man, is adept at calming the skittish amateurs. During the program's long run, he has traveled hundreds of thousands of miles with the show in search of new contestants.

(Top) With announcer Dennis James.

(Above) A three-time winner was Liber Frenkel, an Israeli who imitated Al Jolson.

(Left) Mack is shown here with a group of three-time winners. They are (left to right): The Four Peanuts, a barbershop quartet; baritone Robert Hamilton; violinist Norma Ferris; accordionist Patrick O'Brien; tenor Michael McCarthy; and Myrna and Carolos Camara, Castilian dancers.

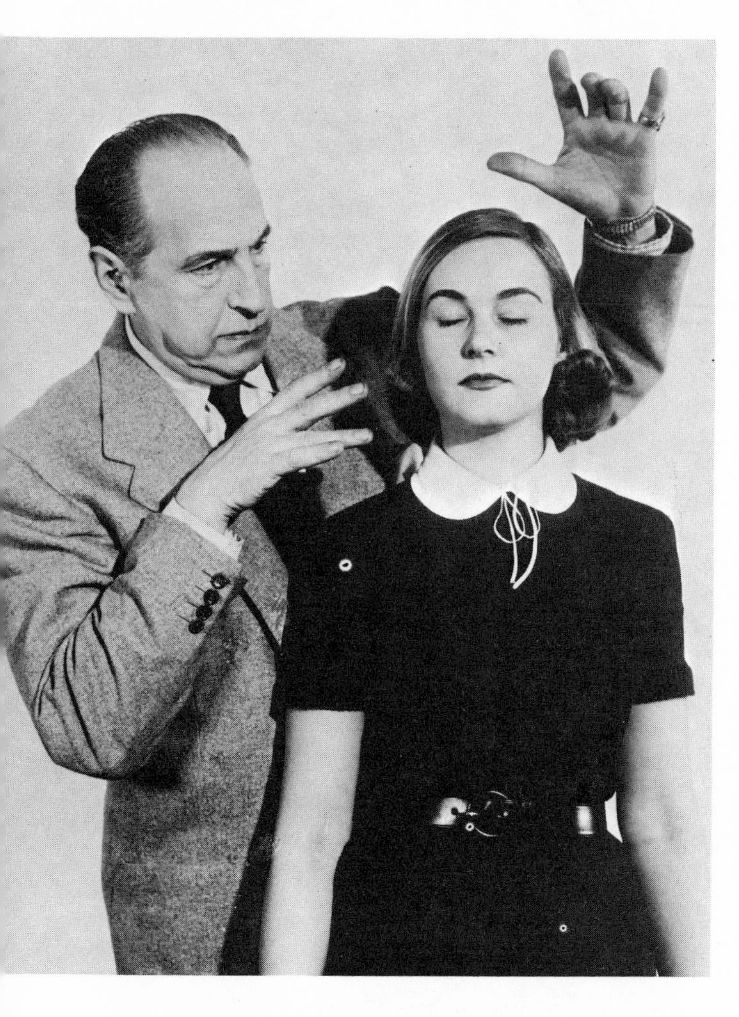

(Above) DUNNINGER: The master mentalist demonstrated his mind-reading act on his own show in 1955. Earlier (1948) he had costarred on *The Bigelow Show* with vertriloquist Paul Winchell.

(Top, right) VINCENT PRICE: In 1958 Price was host of *ESP,* a show designed to demonstrate the existence of extrasensory perception. The show was short-lived, a situation which some attributed to a singular lack of perception on the part of its producers.

(Right) KUDA BUX: *The Kuda Bux Show,* featuring the Indian mentalist, was seen in 1950. He has since made numerous guest appearances, reading sealed messages while his eyes were swathed in blindfolds and several yards of tape and bandages.

(Above) JACK LA LANNE: His is one of the most popular of the exercise-and-keep-fit shows, which have become a staple programming feature on many stations.

(Above) ERN WESTMORE: One of Hollywood's famed Westmore brothers, the beauty-and-makeup consultant presented his own *Ern Westmore Show* in 1953. He is shown here with one audience participant; his wife Betty stands behind him.

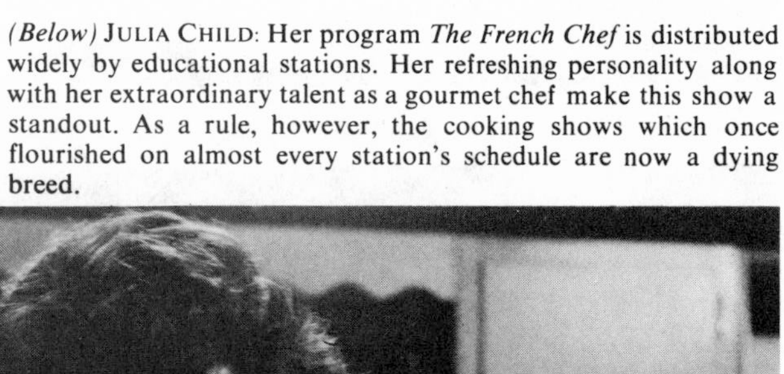

(Below) JULIA CHILD: Her program *The French Chef* is distributed widely by educational stations. Her refreshing personality along with her extraordinary talent as a gourmet chef make this show a standout. As a rule, however, the cooking shows which once flourished on almost every station's schedule are now a dying breed.

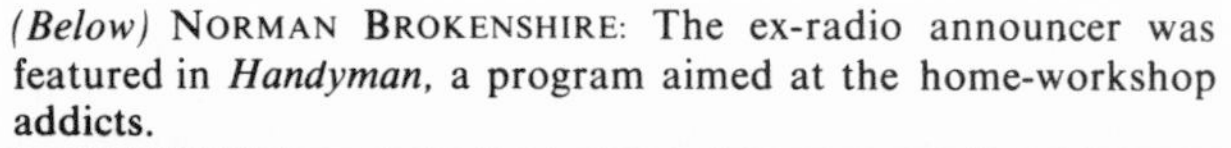

(Below) NORMAN BROKENSHIRE: The ex-radio announcer was featured in *Handyman*, a program aimed at the home-workshop addicts.

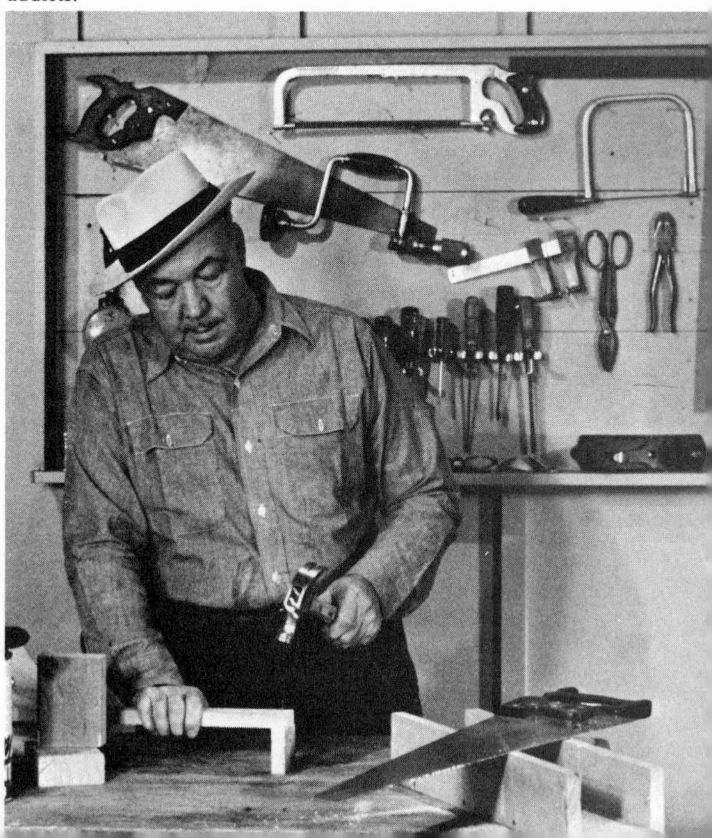

TENNESSEE ERNIE FORD, the peapicker's pal, made his television debut in 1954, heading the old Kay Kyser quiz show *College of Musical Knowledge*. The following year he was at the helm of his own daily variety series, and in 1956 he added a weekly nighttime show. A singer-comedian (his recording of "Sixteen Tons" was one of the top sellers of the decade), Ford specializes in rural-flavored witticisms and has been called a "cracker-barrel Socrates." A daily highlight of his programs is the closing hymn.

(Above) The cast of the daytime *Tennessee Ernie Ford Show* in 1955 included (left to right) singer-announcer Skip Farrell, songstress Doris Drew, Ford, and fifteen-year-old singer Molly Bee.

(Left) On the nighttime variety presentation, *The Ford Show*, in 1958.

(Below) As host (1954) of *College of Musical Knowledge*. Cheerleaders are (left to right) Donna Brown, Spring Mitchell, and Maureen Cassidy.

(Left) ART BAKER: As host of *You Asked for It,* he presented a wide assortment of guests who performed unlikely stunts. Baker is shown here with escape artist Leo Irby ("The Great LeRoy").

(Bottom, left) SHERMAN BILLINGSLEY: *The Stork Club,* which made its debut in 1950, was an attempt to re-create the atmosphere of the then famous (now defunct) cafe. As host, Billingsley moved among the tables, pausing to chat with show-business celebrities and the cream of Cafe Society. The show remained on the air for more than three years.

(Below) DON MCNEILL: *Don McNeill's TV Club* was the video version of "The Breakfast Club," a long-running radio success. Although the cast of the television program was the same as that of the radio show (Fran Allison, right, portrayed "Aunt Fanny"), the television version never achieved a similar popularity.

(Above) PRINCE MONOLULU: Ras Monolulu, a self-styled Ethiopian prince, made a number of appearances on American television. His garb, vocabulary, and title were all colorful indeed, but most appealing was his occupation. Monolulu was an international racetrack tout.

(Top, right) ZACHERLEY: For a period of time in the late fifties a prevailing rage was the local stations' use of live "monsters" to introduce late night movies. Zacherley was an Eastern representative of the genre (first in Philadelphia and then in New York), and differed from many of the others in that he was often deliberately funny. One of his west coast counterparts was a weird young lady who called herself Vampira.

(Right) JOE INTERLIGGI: One of television's most endearing traits is its habit of unearthing strange and wondrous guests. Ranking high in this group was Joe "Iron Jaw" Interliggi, a young vegetarian blessed with a set of powerful mandibles. Interliggi made a number of appearances on Steve Allen's *Tonight* show, and is shown here as a contestant on Groucho Marx's *You Bet Your Life*.

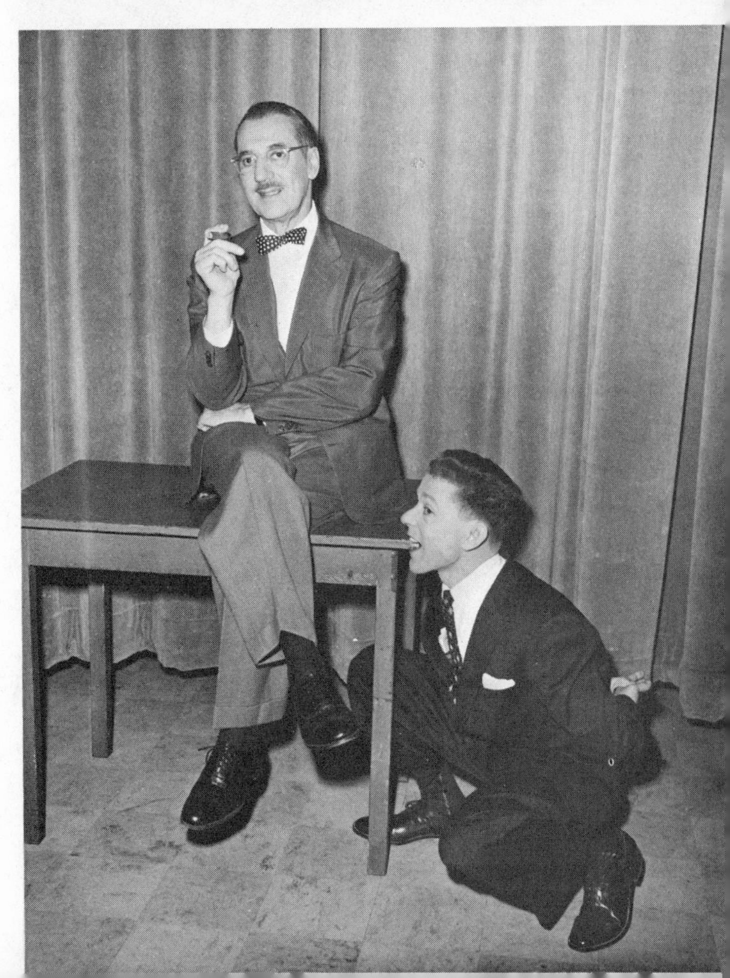

(Above) CANDID CAMERA: Host Allen Funt (shown here with guest Laraine Day) first brought *Candid Camera* to television in 1949; that particular incarnation of the series was broadcast until 1952. *Candid Camera* was the visual version of Funt's radio success "Candid Mike." Its premise is the entrapment of unsuspecting subjects in ludicrous situations. At one time critics regularly lambasted Funt for involving people in embarrassing or humiliating episodes, but such criticism is rarely voiced nowadays. The current rendition of the show regularly includes some charming interviews with young children as well as some beautifully photographed pictorial essays.

(Left) THE HOLLYWOOD PALACE: As its name implies, this is a lavish, gaudy, star-studded re-creation of the great days of vaudeville. Emceed each week by big-name stars (here, Maurice Chevalier), the show rivals Ed Sullivan's with its profusion of acts, many of them well-known and high-priced. The show's list of star-hosts has included Bing Crosby, George Burns, Judy Garland, and Martha Raye.

DAVE GARROWAY
made his first major television contribution with the Chicago-based *Garroway at Large* in 1949. One of the earliest variety programs, its unhurried, low-pitched manner—which reflected Garroway's personality—set the tone for what was to become known as "the Chicago school" of broadcasting. The show ended in 1951 and the following year Garroway came to New York to serve as host of a new concept in television broadcasting, *Today*. *Today* was received coolly by the critics (it suffered, initially, from an overdose of gadgetry), but settled down to become one of the most commercially successful programs in the history of the medium. A potpourri of news, interviews, time-and-weather checks, guest performances, and conversation, the show has beaten back all competitive efforts to curb its dominance of the early-morning hours. For three years (1955–58) Garroway also was host of *Wide Wide World*, which, like *Today*, was one of Sylvester L. "Pat" Weaver's many programming innovations. Since leaving *Today*, Garroway's occasional broadcasting chores have included a series for educational television.

(Above) In 1958 the *Today* lineup of performers looked like this (left to right): sports editor Jack Lescoulie, features editor Charles Van Doren, women's editor Betsy Palmer, news editor Frank Blair, Garroway.

(Top, right) On *Today*'s fifth birthday (in 1956) Garroway celebrates with J. Fred Muggs, the chimp that often upstaged him on the show. Muggs was later dropped from the cast amid insinuations (vehemently denied by his owner-trainer) that he occasionally bit some of the human members of the troupe.

(Right) With Pat Weaver, the innovative NBC executive.

(Bottom, right) The familiar Garroway sign-off—an upraised palm and the single word "Peace."

(Below) The *Garroway at Large* cast included (left to right) Jack Haskell, Cliff Norton, Connie Russell, Garroway, and some members of the show's dancing ensemble.

JOHN CHANCELLOR: Newsman Chancellor was Dave Garroway's successor on *Today.* He later left the show and became director of the Voice of America. Shown here with Chancellor are Frank Blair and Louise O'Brien.

HUGH DOWNS: Chancellor's successor as key man on *Today* was Hugh Downs, who had formerly served as Jack Paar's sidekick on the *Tonight* show. Pictured here are Jack Lescoulie, Downs, Barbara Walters, and Frank Blair.

(Right) WALTER CRONKITE: Among the various shows and hosts which CBS scheduled opposite NBC's *Today* was *The Morning Show* with Walter Cronkite. On this two-hour mélange of music, news, and entertainment, newsman Cronkite was supported by the Bil and Cora Baird puppets, including (right) a lion named Charlemane.

(Bottom, right) WILL ROGERS, JR.: In 1956 *The Morning Show* became *Good Morning!* and featured as host the son of America's most revered humorist.

(Below) MIKE DOUGLAS: *The Mike Douglas Show* attained widespread popularity although it defied television tradition in doing so. Based in Cleveland, it presented a variety format on a much more lavish and creative scale than is usually seen on local stations. In a short time it was being picked up by other stations, and it soon boasted a small network of its own. Starring singer-emcee Douglas, the show features a varied array of guest performers (below, comedian Dick Gregory). In 1966 the show moved to Philadelphia and now has a fresh transfusion of guests shuttling in from the canyons of Manhattan, one hundred miles away.

Broadway Open House was the pioneer late-night variety show. It first appeared in 1950 with Morey Amsterdam as the comedy emcee. A short time later Jerry Lester took over. Featured cast members included Milton Delugg, David Street, Ray Malone, Dagmar, and Wayne Howell. The off-the-cuff, ad-lib nature of *Broadway Open House* gave it a sparkle and spontaneity that were to be emulated by subsequent late-night variety programs. Lester's pixieish humor and his Beanbag Club are still fondly remembered by the show's loyal viewers. *Broadway Open House* departed in 1951 amid rumors of a feud between Lester and Dagmar.

(Above) In a getup reminiscent of Milton Berle, Jerry Lester wields a mop.

(Top, left) In a sketch with Wayne Howell.

(Center, left) Accordionist Milton Delugg (composer of "Orange Colored Sky") was the show's musical director.

(Left) Dagmar, a statuesque blonde whose deadpan poetry renditions were an *Open House* highlight, does a reading with Lester.

Steve Allen

made his debut in 1954 as host of the *Tonight* show, which had begun as a local program a year earlier. It was a wild and woolly variety package which leaned heavily on the multiple talents of its star. The show was a sometimes scripted, sometimes impromptu affair consisting of songs, sketches, interviews, guest stars, and an abundance of offbeat features. Allen remained with the show until 1957 (during the period he also served for two years as a panelist on *What's My Line?*). In 1956 he became the host of the weekly *Steve Allen Show.* More recently he replaced Garry Moore as moderator of *I've Got a Secret,* after serving for several years as host of a non-network variety program based in Holly-

wood. In addition to his comedy work, Allen is a pianist, composer, author of published works of prose and poetry, and political activist. Many of his former cast members (notably Bill Dana, Don Knotts, Steve Lawrence, Eydie Gormé, and Andy Williams) have gone on to establish themselves as stars in their own right.

(Top, right) Cast members of *The Steve Allen Show* (left to right): Dayton Allen, Bill Dana, Louis Nye, Steve Allen, Don Knotts, Pat Harrington, Jr., Gabe Dell. Not shown: Tom Poston, Skitch Henderson.

(Right) "The Question Man" was Allen's answer to a once-popular radio show, "The Answer Man." In this feature Allen provided wacky questions for previously supplied answers.

(Bottom, right) Members of the *Tonight* cast included (left to right) announcer Gene Rayburn, Allen, and singers Eydie Gormé and Steve Lawrence. Singers Andy Williams and Pat Kirby were also show regulars.

(Below) A familiar face in the *Tonight* audience was Mrs. Sterling. She was present at every performance and was a frequent recipient of both gags and gifts (especially some huge salamis,.an Allen trademark). Mrs. Sterling's able successor was a Miss Miller, who attended all of Jack Paar's *Tonight* shows.

JACK PAAR
took over the *Tonight* show in 1957; the following year it was retitled *The Jack Paar Show*. He had previously been the star of four network daytime shows, but was still largely unknown to the television audience. He became a national celebrity through his work on this late-night opus. An emotional man who admitted that he wore his heart on his sleeve, Paar gave a full public airing to all his feuds and friendships, triumphs and disasters. As audiences cheered him on, he lashed out at those he considered unfair to him, notably columnists Walter Winchell and Dorothy Kilgallen. At one point he walked off the stage in mid-show, declaring that the network was censoring him (a questionable joke about a water closet had been blipped from the tape). After a hurried trip to Hong Kong, he was persuaded to return. Paar's forte was conversation, and his programs included hundreds of hilarious chats with Hermione Gingold, Alexander King, Zsa Zsa Gabor, Hans Conried, Cliff Arquette, Peter Ustinov, and many others. There was also one highly charged encounter with Mickey Rooney. Paar left the nightly grind to do a weekly one-hour variety show. This series, too, had its moments (on one occasion, Richard Nixon played the piano); among the features were Paar's own films of his trips to remote areas of the world. Paar now does occasional specials and is active in the management of a television station he owns in Maine.

(Left) For a brief period in 1953 Paar served as quizmaster of *Bank on the Stars*. He is shown here with two contestants.

(Bottom, left) As host of *The Morning Show* in 1954.

(Below) The cast of *The Jack Paar Show* (morning version): Paar, Edie Adams, Richard Hayes, bandleader Pupi Campo.

(Bottom, right) A year later, in 1955, an afternoon version of *The Jack Paar Show* was presented. In the cast were Paar, Jack Haskell, Jose Melis, and Edie Adams.

(Right) Two frequent visitors to the *Tonight* show were comedienne Dody Goodman and chanteuse Genevieve. Paar and Miss Goodman later parted ways; the cause of the split was the subject of much speculation in the press.

(Bottom, right) With singer Trish Dwelley. A minor brouhaha followed Miss Dwelley's appearance on the *Tonight* show. Paar's emotional introduction and misty-eyed reaction to Miss Dwelley's singing was based on the premise that this was her first television performance. It later developed that Miss Dwelley had sung on *The Perry Como Show* and Paar was visibly and publicly upset by the news.

(Below) With a favorite guest, the late Elsa Maxwell.

(Above) LES CRANE: ABC's entry in the late-night sweepstakes was a coltish ex-disc jockey named Les Crane. He strenuously sought controversy on his shows, as well as entertainment. Despite a spankingly modernistic set and such gadgets as a shotgun microphone (see photo), *The Les Crane Show* was canceled in 1965, after only a few months on the air.

(Top, left) TONIGHT: AMERICA AFTER DARK: In January, 1957, after Steve Allen's departure, *Tonight* adopted a new format and a longer title. Jack Lescoulie (right, with Judy Johnson) was the anchor man for the show, which featured newspaper columnists *(center, left)*, including (left to right) Hy Gardner, Earl Wilson, Vernon Scott, Irv Kupcinet, Bob Considine, and Paul Coates. The program was mercilessly drubbed by the columnists' critical brethren and died seven months later.

(Bottom, left) MERV GRIFFIN: An actor and singer ("I've Got a Lovely Bunch of Coconuts") who had emceed several game shows, Griffin substituted occasionally as host on *Tonight* and was favorably received by both audience and critics. The result was *The Merv Griffin Show*, a nightly program owned and distributed (to a large lineup of stations) by Group W (Westinghouse Broadcasting). Like its competitors, the show features talk punctuated by occasional songs and stand-up comedy routines—and every once in a while by an unexpected incident like the moment from a 1966 show pictured here: Broadway producer David Merrick (far right) vehemently states his case to Griffin before walking off the show. Looking on are Renee Taylor, Phil Foster, and Beatrice Lillie.

JOHNNY CARSON,
a young comedian with a great deal of previous television experience, took over as host of *The Tonight Show* in 1962. Unlike Steve Allen, who maintained a frenetic pace, or Jack Paar, who seemed to thrive on moments of emotional crisis, Carson's strong point is his cool, controlled sense of comedy, best evidenced in his conversations with his guests. He is particularly adept at "takes" (comic facial reactions), a technique he uses with devastating results when he finds himself trapped in a piece of especially dreadful comedy material. The show is generally oriented toward entertainment, and most of the guests are show-business personalities. Other program regulars are announcer Ed McMahon, who had served with Carson on *Who Do You Trust?*, and orchestra leader Skitch Henderson, who had occupied the same position when Steve Allen was the show's host.

(*Above*) With guest William Bendix on the daytime *Johnny Carson Show* in 1955.

(*Top, left*) In 1954 Carson (right, with Jackie Loughery) hosted a quiz show called *Earn Your Vacation.*

(*Bottom, left*) As host of the afternoon quiz show *Who Do You Trust?*

(*Below*) On the set of *The Tonight Show* with Skitch Henderson and Ed McMahon.

The Sounds of Music

A TELEVISION SET is a picture box. Television is something you look at, or watch, or view. It is a visual medium. What the sets sound like has been of little concern to their designers or engineers, or to the members of the public, who are referred to as "viewers," not "listeners."

All of this may explain why television, on the whole, has not been kind to people who are supposed to be heard but not necessarily seen. Men and women of music—those who sing it and those who play it—have battled hard to win acceptance on television. Very few of them have scored notable successes.

Among the singers, Perry Como, Dinah Shore, and Andy Williams have fared the best of those who have tried to carry weekly series. And Julie Andrews, Barbra Streisand, Mary Martin, and few more have done well with specials. But Bing Crosby, Frank Sinatra, Judy Garland, Sammy Davis, Jr., and dozens of others whose records and personal appearances have lifted them to the top of the entertainment business have been taken down a peg by that finicky audience out there in television land.

On the other hand, that audience has taken to its bosom a diverse assortment of musical exponents, ranging from Liberace to Dick Clark, from Lawrence Welk to Leonard Bernstein.

Bernstein has managed to break through television's serious-music barrier, but he is the only longhair (with the exception of those who carry electric guitars) who has found anything ap-

CHAPTER III

proaching steady employment on commercial television. Educational television has been a bit more hospitable to serious musicians, but there appears to be no danger that television will undermine concert halls, opera houses, or hi-fi the way it has the movie industry.

Nor has the jazz musician found a congenial outlet for his wares in television. Some of America's finest jazzmen manage to make a buck by playing in television studio orchestras, but the sound of real freewheeling jazz rarely emanates from television-set speakers.

If music is your game, how do you make the grade in television? It's the old story: You gotta have a gimmick. Como didn't just stand around singing—he worked strenuously at acting relaxed while reading words written for him by a platoon of *comedy* writers. Dinah? She got into everybody's act, displayed a magnificent wardrobe, and struggled through intricate production numbers. Bernstein? His shows are more talk than music. Mitch Miller? The name of the game is "Sing Along." Liberace? Well . . .

In other words, showmanship is the key to success. How much of a showman can you be with a violin attached to your chin? Florian ZaBach answered that question. Heifetz couldn't compete.

People simply do not buy their television sets for the purpose of staring at other people singing lieder or blues or rock 'n' roll, or playing harpsichords or banjos or tenor saxes. Those images on the screen have to *move*. If a man stands in one place for too long, or if the camera dwells on him too lingeringly—click!, all over America channels are switched.

Music may have charms, but they have yet to tame television.

Bing Crosby was a guest on several of Como's shows.

PERRY COMO,
Bing Crosby, and Frank Sinatra were the three male pop singers considered most likely to succeed when the newfangled medium of television came along. As it turned out, it was the dark horse of the three, Como, who became the most successful. In fact, no male singer yet has matched the long and prosperous career this ex-barber from Canonsburg, Pennsylvania, has had on television. His relaxed singing style became the butt of comedians' jibes ("Wake up, Perry!"), but it proved to be ideally suited to the intimate, casual atmosphere of television viewing in the home. His easygoing disposition earned him the title "Mr. Nice Guy." He started out in 1948 with *The Chesterfield Supper Club,* which became *The Perry Como Show* in 1950 and ran through 1955, mostly as a thrice-weekly, fifteen-minute series. In 1955 he began a weekly hour-long NBC series which became Saturday night's top-rated show, drove Jackie Gleason (his CBS competition) off the air, and ran until 1963 (in its latter years, on weekday nights, as *The Kraft Music Hall*). The supporting cast included announcer Frank Gallop, Mitch Ayres' orchestra, the Ray Charles Singers, and, at various times, Joey Heatherton, Kaye Ballard, Don Adams, Sandy Stewart, and Milt Kamen. Goodman Ace supervised the scripts. Como quit the weekly grind in 1963 and settled down with a half-dozen specials a year.

The finale of a 1960 Como show (left to right): Bert Lahr, Kay Starr, Como, Anne Brancroft, and the Mills Brothers.

Dinah Shore's television career paralleled Como's in many ways. Of all the ladies of song, only she managed to achieve huge success with a weekly musical series. She began on television in 1951, with early-evening songfests twice a week, alternating with Como's show. In 1956 she tried a couple of hour-long specials masterminded by producer Bob Banner, written by Bob Wells and Johnny Bradford, and choreographed by Tony Charmoli. They were so well received that Miss Shore was given an hour-long weekly show a few months later, with the same production team in charge. The show became one of the most popular on the air—and also one of the most imaginative. Miss Shore's talents and those of her guests were exploited to maximum advantage, camera work was ingenious, and the production numbers were brilliantly conceived and executed. But by 1962 the show's popularity had faded—as had that of musical-variety shows in general—and Miss Shore changed from weekly programs to occasional specials. Through it all, she performed with infectious enthusiasm and an unfailing smile, ending every show with a "Mwah!"—a kiss thrown to the audience (see picture on right).

(Above) UKULELE IKE: Cliff Edwards strummed and sang in his short-lived early show.

(Below) BOB HOWARD: Perry Como and Dinah Shore were the exceptions: pop music on television has, in reality, been one long parade of singers hoping to make a lasting impression on viewers but, in most cases, basking in the television spotlight only briefly. Bob Howard and his show, *Sing It Again,* are remembered only by the owners of the earliest television sets.

(Above) JOHN CONTE: His *Little Show* was big in the early days. Conte later became the non-singing host of *Matinee Theatre.*

(Below) VAUGHN MONROE: His *Camel Caravan* was on the air in 1950 and 1951, and Monroe had another series in the summer of 1954. But his most profitable television venture was his stint delivering commercials for RCA.

(Left) KATE SMITH: For many years a radio star, Kate Smith started on television with a daily late-afternoon show in 1950, then added a weekly evening hour in 1951. Her shows had run their course by 1954. Miss Smith returned briefly in 1960 with a new weekly series, but has appeared on television infrequently since then.

(Center, left) ROSEMARY CLOONEY: Her first big television break came on *Songs for Sale* in 1950. A few months later she joined the cast of *The Robert Q. Lewis Matinee.* In 1956 she did *The Rosemary Clooney Show,* a syndicated series (she is shown here in one episode, with The Hi-Lo's). In 1957–58 it was *The Lux Show Starring Rosemary Clooney,* a network series. She has been much in demand for guest appearances ever since.

(Bottom, left) ROBERTA QUINLAN: She became television's most familiar songstress in 1949.

(Below) KYLE MACDONNELL: Most of the women singers, too, have had only brief flings on television. Kyle MacDonnell was one of the first to be "discovered" and turned into a celebrity by television. Her shows, *Girl About Town* and *Celebrity Time,* were viewers' favorites in 1948 and 1949.

(Above) PEGGY LEE and MEL TORME: These two jazz-oriented singers worked together early in the game and have appeared separately on numerous shows since then.

(Below) BILLY DANIELS: The "Old Black Magic" man had his own network series on Sunday evenings in 1952.

(Above) JOHNNY DUGAN: The daytime *Johnny Dugan Show* (1952) featured songs by Dugan and Barbara Logan, and audience-participation stunts.

(Below) JOHNNY JOHNSTON: In 1951 he had his own daytime show as well as singing weekly on *The Ken Murray Show.* Later on he branched out and became a *Masquerade Party* panelist, a regular on *Home,* and host of *Make That Spare,* a bowling show that filled time after boxing telecasts.

(Top) DOTTY MACK: She performed pantomimes to other people's records, first on a local Cincinnati series, then on network shows. □ *(Above)* JO STAFFORD: She has had a few television flings—most recently a series of stylish specials filmed in London and syndicated to quite a few U.S. stations—and has made many guest appearances. □ *(Below)* MINDY CARSON: In 1949 it was *Mindy Carson Sings;* in 1950, a thirteen-week stay as Perry Como's guest; in 1951, *The Ford Star Revue,* with Jack Haley; and in 1952, *Club Embassy.*

(Above) MARTHA WRIGHT: Her fifteen-minute *Packard Showroom* was seen Sunday nights in 1954. Bobby Hackett's cornet played behind her. In 1956 Miss Wright was a featured vocalist on Jack Paar's daytime show. □ *(Below)* BETTY CLOONEY: She substituted for her older sister, Rosemary, on *The Robert Q. Lewis Matinee* in 1950. Jack Paar hired her for his early-morning show in 1954, but fired her and bandleader Pupi Campo in 1955, for reasons which were never explained but which reportedly stemmed from the romance between Miss Clooney and Campo (they subsequently married). After leaving Paar, she hooked on again with *The Robert Q. Lewis Matinee.* □ *(Bottom)* PATTI PAGE: In the early fifties she made a series of syndicated films and appeared on *The Scott Music Hall.* In 1957 she became hostess of *The Big Record,* and a year later was the star of *The Oldsmobile Show,* a low-key, high-quality musical series.

Frank Sinatra
has left an indelible mark through his performances on records, in nightclubs, in concerts, and in movies, but for some reason television success eluded him for years. He tried and failed twice with his own weekly series (1950–52 and 1957–58). He did guest shots on other people's shows. He headlined specials of his own. But it was not until recently that he found the right television setting for those talents which show to such advantage in other media. In the winter of 1965 he offered an hour-long television concert, "Frank Sinatra—A Man and His Music"—just Sinatra alone, singing as nobody else can. This was a Sinatra who had never been seen on television, free from the gimmicks, the inside jokes, the fawning of cronies, and the studied indifference that had previously erected a barrier between him and the television audience. He was, as he should have been all along, Frank Sinatra, singer.

(Top, right) The early days.

(Below) His own show in 1957.

(Bottom, right) As Dean Martin's guest on *Ford Startime* in 1959.

(Above) ERIN O'BRIEN: She was a television discovery, introduced by Steve Allen in 1956. She later worked with Liberace, Frank Sinatra, and Eddie Fisher, as well as in straight acting roles.

(Top, left) GEORGIA GIBBS: Billed as "Her Nibs, Miss Georgia Gibbs," she had a fifteen-minute weekly series called *Georgia Gibbs' Million Record Show* in 1957.

(Center) JAYE P. MORGAN: She sang on *Stop the Music* and with Robert Q. Lewis and was the summer replacement for Eddie Fisher's *Coke Time* in 1956.

(Bottom, left) INA RAY HUTTON: During the summer of 1956, she sang and led her all-girl band as star of a weekly show.

(Below) JILL COREY: She started with Dave Garroway in 1953, moved on to Johnny Carson's weekly series in 1955, *The Robert Q. Lewis Show* the following year, and *Your Hit Parade* in 1957.

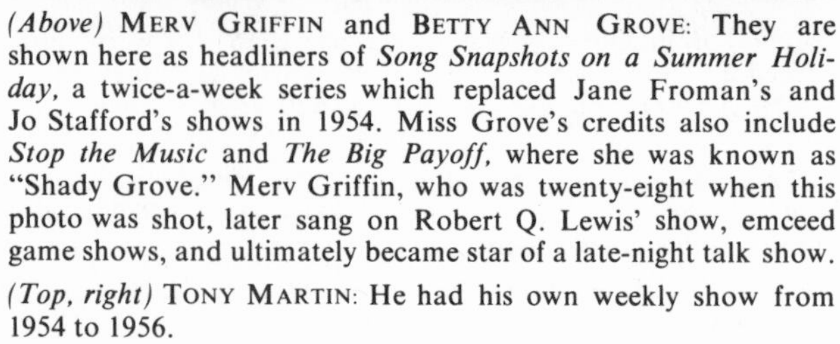

(Above) MERV GRIFFIN and BETTY ANN GROVE: They are shown here as headliners of *Song Snapshots on a Summer Holiday,* a twice-a-week series which replaced Jane Froman's and Jo Stafford's shows in 1954. Miss Grove's credits also include *Stop the Music* and *The Big Payoff,* where she was known as "Shady Grove." Merv Griffin, who was twenty-eight when this photo was shot, later sang on Robert Q. Lewis' show, emceed game shows, and ultimately became star of a late-night talk show.

(Top, right) TONY MARTIN: He had his own weekly show from 1954 to 1956.

(Right) DENNIS DAY: He never could make up his mind whether to concentrate on singing or comedy. His 1952–54 series had a little of each, plus visits from people like Ann Blyth (shown here). Day, of course, also appeared frequently on Jack Benny's show.

(Bottom, right) FRANKIE LAINE: He also had a weekly show in the mid-fifties, and he served as Arthur Godfrey's summer replacement in 1955.

(Below) HOAGY CARMICHAEL: The songwriter-singer was star and host of the ninety-minute *Saturday Night Revue* in 1953. He turned up later in a western, *Laramie.*

JUDY GARLAND arrived on television in 1955, starring in the opening episode of *Ford Star Jubilee*. For ninety minutes she sang, danced, and swapped small talk with David Wayne, while the largest audience ever to watch a spectacular (as the big shows were called in those days) looked on. Her next show was scheduled for 1957, but she walked out on it and a CBS contract after what was described as a dispute over the format. It was not until 1962 that Miss Garland patched up her differences with CBS and returned to television in a special (with Frank Sinatra and Dean Martin as guests) that won raves from the reviewers. She did another special in 1963, then went for broke in September of that year with a weekly Sunday-night series telecast opposite television's top-rated show, *Bonanza*. Her show was in trouble from the outset—producers came and went, the format kept changing, CBS's panicky masterminds shuttled back and forth between the Garland set in Los Angeles and network headquarters in New York—while *Bonanza* rode blithely on, trampling Garland in the ratings. In the spring of 1964, Judy Garland gave up her attempt to tame television and went back to concert halls and nightclubs, where her unique talents found a more appreciative audience.

(Below) Rehearsing for her television debut in 1955.

(Top, left) Rehearsing again in 1957 for the show that never came off.

(Left) On the air in 1964.

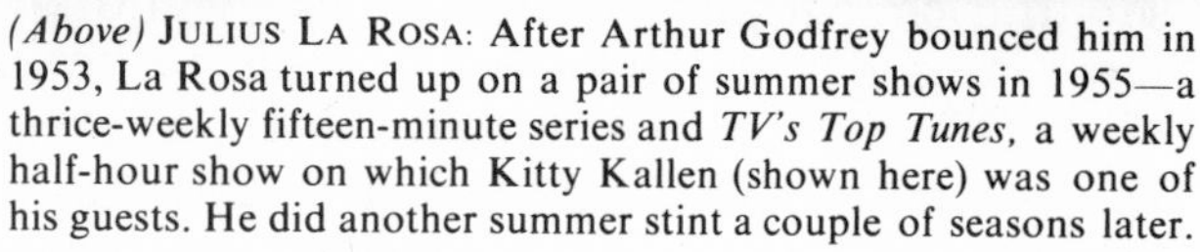

(Above) Julius La Rosa: After Arthur Godfrey bounced him in 1953, La Rosa turned up on a pair of summer shows in 1955—a thrice-weekly fifteen-minute series and *TV's Top Tunes,* a weekly half-hour show on which Kitty Kallen (shown here) was one of his guests. He did another summer stint a couple of seasons later.

(Below) Bing Crosby: Like many performers who were on top of the movie and radio heaps, Crosby has never quite reached the same heights in television. He has done just about everything: situation comedy *(The Bing Crosby Show),* a musical play ("High Tor"), emcee chores *(The Hollywood Palace),* sports (the Bing Crosby Golf Tournament, telecast annually), several specials, and guest appearances on virtually every variety series. Here he is, insouciant as always, accompanied by Buddy Cole.

Eddie Fisher: He made some guest appearances on television before he was drafted in 1951. During his two years in the army he managed to get onto television occasionally, making periodic appearances on *Jane Froman's U.S.A. Canteen* (top). After his discharge he starred on *Coke Time* (above) twice a week from 1953 to 1957. In the fall of 1957 he began a new series of hour-long shows, alternating as star with George Gobel. Debbie Reynolds, his wife at that time, joined him on the air occasionally (below).

(Above) EDIE ADAMS: Her first television appearances were on the local Philadelphia and New York shows conducted by Ernie Kovacs, who later became her husband. In 1955 she sang for Jack Paar on *The Morning Show*, then rejoined Kovacs in 1956 on his network morning show. She branched out into specials and, in 1962, after Kovacs' death, had her own weekly series, *Here's Edie*, on which, among other things, she performed a Kabuki sketch with Maury Wills of the Los Angeles Dodgers.

(Below) GISELE MACKENZIE: An alumna of *Your Hit Parade*, she too had her own show in 1957–58. She also played Sid Caesar's wife for a season.

(Above) PATRICE MUNSEL: She had a weekly show during the 1957–58 season.

(Below) JOHN RAITT and JANET BLAIR: In 1958 and 1959, this duo served together as Dinah Shore's summer replacement. Each of them, separately, has done many guest shots and specials. Miss Blair, too, played Sid Caesar's wife for a while.

(Above) NAT KING COLE: His network show in 1957–58 became a cause celebre. No sponsor was willing to underwrite the show nationally, and it was dropped, despite attempts of many high-priced stars to keep it going by offering to appear on it without remuneration.

(Below) GORDON MACRAE: He was the singing host of *The Colgate Comedy Hour* in 1954 (as pictured) and had his own series two years later.

(Top) CHARLIE APPLEWHITE: Milton Berle discovered this young Texan in 1953. But an army hitch, beginning in 1956, interrupted his promising career, and he never regained the momentum. He faded from sight until he hit the comeback trail in 1966.

(Above) GUY MITCHELL: He was the star of a 1957 musical series.

(Below) TONY BENNETT: His biggest opportunity came in 1958, when he replaced Perry Como for part of the summer.

DEAN MARTIN
was on his own after his split with Jerry Lewis in 1956, and for quite some time the going was rough. He did a few television specials and appeared on various variety shows. An acting role in a movie, "The Young Lions," gave his career a strong push. By 1965 he was a big enough star to dictate terms to the network that wanted him for a weekly vaudeville series. The terms include freedom to do the show with a minimum of preparation. Martin does not show up until the day of the taping, then wanders lackadaisically and engagingly through the show.

(Left) A 1957 appearance on *Club Oasis.*

(Bottom, left) With Robert Goulet, who during the mid-sixties sang on everybody's show and starred in a spy series, *Blue Light.*

(Below) Martin on his own show in 1965, with Louis Armstrong.

(Above) ROY ROGERS: Although he has not had a regular series since the early sixties, Rogers still gets bookings (usually with his wife Dale Evans) on variety shows. During the summer of 1959, when this photo was shot, he appeared on *The Chevy Show* with Eddy Arnold (left) and Audie Murphy.

(Top, right) EDDY ARNOLD: One of the leading western troubadors, he has had his own network series on two occasions.

(Right) GRAND OLE OPRY: Country-and-western music has always found an audience—in more sections of the country than most people realize. The capital of country music is Nashville, Tennessee, where *Grand Ole Opry* was born and is still making money for people like Minnie Pearl (shown here). *Opry* was a national television fixture for years.

(Bottom, right) OZARK JUBILEE: A leading practitioner of this musical genre is Red Foley (left, with Marvin Rainwater), whose *Ozark Jubilee* (it was later called *Country Music Jubilee* and *Jubilee U.S.A.*) had a long network run.

(Below) PEE WEE KING: He presided weekly over ninety minutes of country music and comedy from Cleveland. Singer Goldie Hill (shown here with King) was a guest performer.

(Below) PAT BOONE: The kid in the white-buck shoes got his first exposure on *Arthur Godfrey's Talent Scouts,* became a member of Godfrey's television "family," then went off on his own in 1957. *The Pat Boone Show* ran for several seasons. When it ended, Boone went on to movies, though he continued to make guest appearances on television.

(Above) JIMMY DEAN: He succeeded in striking a happy medium between western music and pop—his show had the flavor of corn, but was seasoned with enough sophistication to make it palatable to its intensely loyal viewers. As a result, the hour-long *Jimmy Dean Show* survived many threats of cancellation before it finally perished in 1966. Dean, a Texan, got his start in Washington, D.C., then went network in 1957. This photo was taken in 1959, when he had a daytime series (The Noteworthies and Jeri Miyazaki are singing along with him).

Your Hit Parade
was a phenomenon of television all through the fifties. It began in 1950 with the top seven tunes of the week plus some old-time "Lucky Strike Extras." As the years passed, the show did fewer and fewer current tunes and more and more extras. All through its run, *Your Hit Parade* featured inventive production numbers, staged first by Tony Charmoli and later by Ernie Flatt and Peter Gennaro. They *had* to be inventive because the same tuneless hits stayed on top of the charts for long periods, and new gimmicks were needed week after week to illustrate these tired songs. The original cast included Eileen Wilson, Snooky Lanson, and Dorothy Collins. In 1952 the personnel were as pictured here (from left): Russell Arms (in sweater), June Valli, Snooky Lanson, Dorothy Collins, and Raymond Scott (musical director and Miss Collins' husband). Gisele MacKenzie replaced Miss Valli in 1953. In 1957, as ratings sagged, the entire cast was purged and Tommy Leonetti, Jill Corey, Alan Copeland, and Virginia Gibson were brought in. In 1958 a $200,000 mystery-tune contest was introduced as an added inducement to viewers. Neither of these moves worked. The show went off, but returned under new management in 1959, with Dorothy Collins and Johnny Desmond starred. On April 24, 1959, it breathed its last. The three top tunes that night were "Come Softly to Me," "Venus," and "Pink Shoelaces," typical of the type of music that had stomped *Your Hit Parade* to death—rock 'n' roll.

DICK CLARK: The Robespierre of the music revolution that overthrew shows like *Your Hit Parade* was a clean-cut, well-spoken young chap named Dick Clark, who rose from the obscurity of Philadelphia disc-jockeydom to the position of national arbiter of popular-music fashions. It was never quite clear whether he knew instinctively what teen-agers would like or whether they mindlessly liked whatever he told them to, but Clark had the power to make stars of the likes of Fabian, Frankie Avalon, Paul Anka, and (shown here, on right, with Clark) Chubby Checker. Clark's platform was *American Bandstand,* a daily dance party which began in 1957 and was soon joined by a weekly nighttime version. By 1963 *Bandstand* had been reduced to a once-a-week show and Clark, by now an elder statesman of the Pepsi Generation, moved on to more dignified pursuits, such as emceeing game shows.

THE ARTHUR MURRAY PARTY: A different type of dance party had an extraordinary run through the fifties and into the sixties. Its hostess was a rank amateur (she admitted it freely), Kathryn Murray, who advised viewers to "Put a little fun in your life—try dancing." Her husband Arthur seconded the motion, while impassively enduring barrages of insults from comedians. *The Arthur Murray Party* started in 1950, with skits, dancing lessons, and contests. It was on and off the air countless times, usually as a summer series, until it really came into its own in the 1958–59 season, when, defying all rational analysis, it became one of the most popular programs on the air. Soon afterward it was canceled, as it had been so many times before. But only the most foolhardy prophet would predict that television has seen the last of this remarkably resilient show.

ANDY WILLIAMS,
an unprepossessing crooner from Wall Lake, Iowa, has, more successfully than any of his television contemporaries, managed to withstand the rapid changes in musical tastes. In alpaca sweater and sporty hat, he has kept rolling along, singing a song, and proving that the much-beleaguered musical-variety format is not dead. Steve Allen introduced him to television audiences in 1954 on the *Tonight* show. In 1957 he did the twice-a-week bit, costarring with June Valli. He became a much-sought-after summer replacement, substituting for Pat Boone in 1958 and for Garry Moore in 1959. His day came in 1962, when he got his own weekly series. It was cut back to twelve shows a year in 1963, but in 1964 Williams went weekly again, settling down for what looked like a long stay.

(Left) The Andy Williams Show is a relaxed, low-pressure hour.

(Bottom, left) In 1957 it was *The Andy Williams-June Valli Show.*

(Below) The next summer he replaced Pat Boone on *The Chevy Showroom.* (The blonde is Gail Kuhr, the brunette Jayne Turner.)

LIBERACE
(full name: Wladziu Valentino Liberace) had a mouthful of luminescent teeth, a scalp full of wavy blond hair, a silky voice, sequin-festooned costumes, and a flamboyant piano style which placed as much emphasis on how the pianist looked as on how he sounded. He also had, throughout the fifties, an idolatrous audience consisting mostly of older women who apparently felt the urge to mother him (many of them, for some reason, felt the same way about the wrestler Gorgeous George, whom in some ways Liberace resembled). He started with a Los Angeles television show in 1951, went national in 1952, and began filming a syndicated series in 1953, making more than one hundred episodes, which were shown by stations all over the country. An imitation Louis XIV candelabra always graced Liberace's piano, and his brother George, a violinist, led the orchestra which accompanied him. All celebrities are subjected to ridicule, but none more vicious than that which was directed at Liberace. He accepted most of it with good grace (though he did sue a British columnist, Cassandra, for libel). Indeed, he seemed to thrive on it. His favorite answer to his critics was: "I cried all the way to the bank."

(Below) FLORIAN ZABACH: He called himself "the poet of the violin." When it came to speed, he was unexcelled—he could play the 1,280 notes of "Hora Staccato" in one hundred seconds. Since fiddling has never been recognized as an Olympic event, he had to content himself with a television career, making guest appearances with Milton Berle, Ken Murray, and Steve Allen, then launching his own series in 1954. He was assisted on his show by the "pixie ballerina," Mary Ellen Terry.

(Above) Paul Whiteman: Some orchestra leaders have ventured into television too. One of the pioneers was Paul Whiteman, who not only conducted several television series (a talent contest called *On the Boardwalk* when this photo was shot), but also served as ABC's vice president in charge of music.

(Above) Eddie Condon: A different brand of music was dished out by jazzman Eddie Condon and assorted sidemen on *Floor Show* when television was young. Pictured here are Wild Bill Davison on cornet and Cutty Cuttshall on trombone.

(Below) Fred Waring: For five years, beginning in 1949, *The Fred Waring Show* was a Sunday-night television staple. Waring did some specials during the 1954–55 season and had a daytime series during the summer of 1957.

(Below) Kay Kyser: His *College of Musical Knowledge* was around in the early fifties, with Ish Kabbible providing the comic relief. Ernie Ford took over the show after Kyser retired.

(Above) BOB CROSBY: This bandleader gave up the band and became the singing host of *The Bob Crosby Show,* a daytime musical series.

(Top, left) THE DORSEY BROTHERS: Jimmy (left) and Tommy Dorsey were brought to television by Jackie Gleason. They replaced Gleason's show for a couple of weeks during the summer of 1954. In the fall of 1955 they took to the air regularly, as co-hosts of *Stage Show,* which shared an hour-long time slot with Gleason's *The Honeymooners.* Elvis Presley made his television debut on *Stage Show.*

(Left) SAMMY KAYE: He starred in *So You Want to Lead a Band* in 1954 (Jeffrey Clay is the vocalist here) and *Sammy Kaye's Music from Manhattan* in 1958.

(Bottom, left) SPIKE JONES: He played it for laughs on several shows and his wife, Helen Grayco, sang along with the gags.

(Below) HORACE HEIDT: This show was called *Swift Show Wagon with Horace Heidt and the American Way.* On the air in 1954 and 1955, it featured a talent contest and a salute to a different state every week.

(Above) XAVIER CUGAT: His Latin rhythms have been heard often on television, in his own shows and in appearances with Ed Sullivan, Steve Allen, and others. When he was married to Abbe Lane (shown here), she always worked with him.

(Below) GUY LOMBARDO: He was joined by his brothers in various television ventures, including, in 1956, *Guy Lombardo's Diamond Jubilee,* featuring a letter-writing contest; and annual New Year's Eve telecasts. The Lombardos (left to right) are Lebert, Carmen, Victor, and Guy.

(Above) RAY ANTHONY: He had a summer series in 1956. Here he rehearses with Molly Bee, who had been a regular on Ernie Ford's show and later sang frequently on Jimmy Dean's.

(Below) BUDDY BREGMAN: *The Music Shop Starring Buddy Bregman* was a network show in 1959. Bregman subsequently became a major figure in British television.

(Bottom) RUSS MORGAN: He put on a summer show in 1956, aided by singer Helen O'Connell. Miss O'Connell also spent some time as a regular on the *Today* show.

LAWRENCE WELK
is the only orchestra leader who has had a long-lived success on television. His "Champagne Music" has been burping along since 1955 and appears to have become a permanent part of the television scene. Critics have derided the show for years, musicians have knocked the music, comedians have mocked the tongue-tied maestro's "a-one and a-two" song introductions, but the show and its leader have continued to please a substantial portion of the population. Welk's explanation: "Mother likes our music."

(Left) Jazzman Pete Fountain remained relatively subdued when he was a member of Welk's orchestra.

(Bottom, left) Welk's singing group was The Lennon Sisters. Here are three of the five: Kathy, Peggy, and Janet.

(Below) Here he dances with the original "Champagne Lady," Alice Lon. Welk later fired her, because, said Miss Lon, her knees had been visible to the television audience once too often.

MITCH MILLER

exhorted viewers at home to "sing along," and for half a decade they did just that, by the millions. It all started in 1960 when a *Ford Startime* hour was turned over to Miller, whose "Sing Along" record albums were best sellers. After the show NBC was besieged with requests for more of Mitch. In January of 1961 the network found a spot for him, and he did seven shows. Viewer enthusiasm was stronger than ever, and Miller got a weekly series the next fall. Its main components were an all-male, mostly middle-aged chorus, chosen for sound, not for sex appeal; girl vocalists such as Leslie Uggams, Diana Trask, and Gloria Lambert, chosen for both; the simplest, most familiar melodies in ASCAP's catalogues; and Miller's beard, effervescence, and herky-jerky conducting. By 1964, however, the novelty had worn off, and Mitch and his bouncing ball left the air. But not for good—reruns of some of the shows were broadcast in 1966.

LEONARD BERNSTEIN
did not ask viewers to sing along, but rather to listen, learn, and enjoy. Though he did not hesitate to delve into popular music, his subject was more likely to be a symphony, a sonata, a concerto, or an opera. Bernstein, who had achieved mastery over the piano, orchestra conducting, composition, and musical comedy before his hair turned gray, has dominated the presentation of serious music on television. He has made his mark as much with words as with music. An extraordinarily articulate and lucid lecturer, he arrived on the television scene in November of 1954, when *Omnibus* gave the thirty-six-year-old Bernstein half an hour to explain Beethoven's "Fifth Symphony." He did it so effectively that he was asked to lecture on other aspects of music, and he has done so—with the aid of the New York Philharmonic, various soloists, and his piano—ever since, several times a year. His *Young People's Concerts* began in 1958, and most seasons he has conducted an adult series of specials as well.

(Above) On *Omnibus* in 1956.

(Below) He traveled to Tokyo in 1962 and filmed a performance of gagaku—the symphonic music of ancient Japan—played by the Imperial Court Musicians.

(Bottom, right) In 1959 Bernstein did a Christmas special with England's celebrated St. Paul's Cathedral Boys' Choir.

(Above) VOICE OF FIRESTONE: Outside of Bernstein's programs, there has been little room for serious music on television. *Voice of Firestone* survived for fourteen years on television (after twenty-one years on radio), presenting classics and semiclassics to a small but fervent segment of the television audience. In 1963, despite protests from viewers and some government officials, *Firestone* was canceled. The show's longtime conductor was Howard Barlow (right), here greeting baritone Thomas L. Thomas.

(Below) THE BELL TELEPHONE HOUR: Classical music has been offered by this series too—it has been on the air in one form or another since 1959—but pop, show, folk, and jazz tunes are usually sprinkled liberally among the more serious musical pieces. Here is one show's cast: violinist Zino Francescatti, ballerina Nina Novak, musical-comedy star Alfred Drake, jazz trumpeter Red Nichols, Broadway star Sally Ann Howes, and, at the piano, pop vocalist Connee Boswell. Their 1959 show also featured a folk-singing group, the Kingston Trio. A typical *Telephone Hour* mixture.

(Above) OSCAR LEVANT: Many of the world's finest musicians have been seen on television. Oscar Levant, however, became known to television audiences not as a pianist but as a talk-show host and guest and as a devout neurotic. Before that he spent a summer starring on a panel-variety show, *General Electric Guest House,* shown here.

(Below) ARTUR RUBINSTEIN: He performed on *Meet the Masters* in television's early days.

(Bottom) MISCHA ELMAN: He played on *Saturday Night Revue.*

(Top) MARIAN ANDERSON: The great contralto has made a number of appearances on television. Here she rehearses for 1953's *Ford 50th Anniversary Show.* She was also the subject of a memorable *See It Now* documentary.

(Above) IGOR STRAVINSKY: He has appeared with Bernstein and as conductor of a Stravinsky-Balanchine ballet depicting Noah and the Flood and, here, conducting a concert shown on educational television.

(Below) JOAN SUTHERLAND: She gave a recital on educational television in the mid-sixties.

(Above) THE LIVELY ONES: Popular music has adopted various guises in recent years. This was a brightly original summer series in 1962 and 1963. Vic Damone was its star, and he was accompanied by two girls called Tiger (Joan Staley) and Charley (Shirley Yelm). They were upstaged by first-class singers and musicians, who performed in odd settings or amid offbeat visual effects devised by director Barry Shear. Here is Benny Goodman and his sextet swinging at the Capitol in Washington.

(Top, right) SAMMY DAVIS, JR.: The versatile performer was given his own weekly show in 1966, but it got off to an unfortunate start with a pointless show in which Elizabeth Taylor and Richard Burton joined Davis, and the series lasted only a few months before reruns of *Sing Along with Mitch* replaced it. Trini Lopez sang along with Sammy on one of his shows.

(Right) MAX MORATH: What Leonard Bernstein did for classical music, Morath did for *The Ragtime Era* in his educational-television series.

(Bottom, right) THE KING FAMILY: There were thirty-six of them, all singing at the top of their lungs. A guest shot on *The Hollywood Palace* in 1964 led to their own weekly show, which ran until January, 1966. These are the six King Sisters: Donna, Alyce, Luise, Maxine, Yvonne, and Marilyn.

(Below) HOOTENANNY: College campuses provided the settings for this series, which emphasized folk music but also presented acts like Stan Rubin's Tigertown Five (shown here).

HULLABALOO: The arrival of the discothèque, the Frug, and "a go-go" was celebrated by television primarily in two shows which debuted during the 1964–65 season. One was *Hullabaloo,* which lasted into 1966. Emanating from New York, it featured various bizarre guest performers and (pictured here) the Hullabaloo Dancers. On the far left is Lada Edmund, Jr., whose tremors as the show's "Girl in the Cage" made her a favorite of many viewers. (It was reported that a popular pastime of college students was watching the *Hullabaloo* girls wriggle and writhe, in color—with the sound turned off.)

SHINDIG: Like *Hullabaloo, Shindig* was a frenetic item populated by assorted wailers and twangers, a kicky chorus line, and a screamy audience. It originated in Hollywood. The archives contain no documentation of this, but it may well be that the gentlemen pictured here were the only male performers on *Shindig* who had ever been inside a barber shop. These are four singing members of the Los Angeles Rams' defensive platoon in 1964: Roosevelt Grier (seated), and (from left) Merlin Olsen, David Jones, and Lamar Lundy. Like so many other manifestations of passing musical fancies, *Hullabaloo* and *Shindig* did not survive for long in the mass medium of television.

Custom-Made Comedy

IN THE EARLY YEARS OF TELEVISION, the situation comedy was typified by a single quality: believability. It did not matter whether the accent was on situation (as in *Mama* or *The Goldbergs*) or on comedy (as in *I Love Lucy* or *The Phil Silvers Show*). Nor did it matter that the characters might behave in a bizarre or outlandish fashion; there was a central core of truth and credibility which was easily identified by the audience. It was as though the screen were a mirror, and the viewer could always catch a glimpse —often slightly distorted—of himself. Even a caricature like Chester A. Riley contained a shred of believability; the awe-inspiring, authoritarian figure of the American father *had* eroded, even if it had not become the lump of helpless stupidity Riley portrayed.

In later years, situation comedies came to dominate television programming, representing as they did an excellent means to keep viewers occupied, if not mentally engaged. And if viewers were not necessarily amused, the ratings showed that they were not mutinous either. And so hour after hour, day after day, situation comedies came and went, endless rows of them, spawned of expediency and nourished by apathy. They were the sand dunes in Newton Minow's vast wasteland. Most of the personnel in television found themselves involved in the process of cranking out new situation comedies, and as the pace accelerated, believability all but vanished. The characters became pasteboard figures, with

CHAPTER IV

only their dress and speech to identify them as members of the human race. Plots had little inherent value except as a means to move the program toward the closing commercial. Creativity seemed to end once an occupation had been chosen for the major character in the series. (Only a few choice occupations remain unplumbed. If a way is ever found to rid us of our squeamishness about skin blemishes, we can surely expect a situation comedy about a dermatologist.)

No audience is present during the production of most situation comedies, with the result that no natural audience reaction appears on the finished film or tape. Instead, a laugh track is dubbed in. Thus a contemporary situation comedy consists of artificial characters in artificial situations being egged on by artificial laughter. From time to time, letters appear in magazines and newspapers complaining that some viewers resent maniacal laughter unaccompanied by anything even remotely funny. These complaints probably represent a minority viewpoint; presumably the cast, the producer, and most of the audience welcome the faked hysteria on the grounds that it provides reassurance that what is being perpetrated is indeed comedy.

An occasional rose blooms in the wasteland. A show appears, peopled with recognizable humans who do or say recognizably funny things. They are evidence that all is not irretrievably lost. It is still possible to create a situation comedy inhabited by humans, or reasonable facsimiles thereof, who can evoke genuine laughter. Though the industry relies on assembly lines, the craftsman still survives.

I LOVE LUCY,
starring Lucille Ball and her husband Desi Arnaz, made its debut in 1951. The program was destined to become the most popular in the history of American television. Arnaz, a Cuban bandleader, played Ricky Ricardo, a Cuban bandleader; Miss Ball portrayed a loving wife with a habit of getting involved in all sorts of difficulties and misunderstandings. Their neighbors, Fred and Ethel Mertz, were played by William Frawley and Vivian Vance. Although it was immensely successful, the show lost its first sponsor, a cigarette company, apparently because the program was not helping the sale of the product. *I Love Lucy* had no difficulty in finding other sponsors, none of whom had any complaints about the show's value as a commercial vehicle. The show was produced by Desilu, a company jointly owned by Miss Ball and Arnaz. Following their divorce, Miss Ball retained sole ownership of Desilu, which had become a large and profitable Hollywood production organization. In recent years, Miss Ball has been starring in *The Lucy Show* (with Vivian Vance), but films of the classic *I Love Lucy* series are still rerun endlessly on stations throughout the world.

(Above) The cast of *I Love Lucy* in 1955 during the show's fourth season included (left to right) Vivian Vance, William Frawley, Desi Arnaz, and Lucille Ball.

(Bottom, left) Lucy and her son, Desiderio Alberto Arnaz IV, who was born in 1953. The baby's counterpart on the show, Ricky, Jr., joined the cast at exactly the same time as Lucy's real son was born.

(Below) Crossed eyes and putty nose are Lucy's disguise in this sequence with William Holden in 1955.

(Above) As Cleopatra (in this segment Caesar was portrayed by Hans Conried).

(Top, right) With Orson Welles, who played a magician in this 1956 show.

(Bottom, right) In this 1964 scene from *The Lucy Show* Vivian Vance aids in the search for a contact lens lost in the icing of a chocolate cake.

(Below) Lucy joins a symphony orchestra.

MAMA: Based on a successful play (which, in turn, had been based on a book), this family series featured (left to right) Robin Morgan as Dagmar, Peggy Wood as Mama, Dick Van Patten as Nels, Rosemary Rice as Katrin, and Judson Laire as Papa. *Mama* made its debut in 1949 and remained on the air for eight years. It set the style for many other domestic comedies which followed.

LIFE WITH FATHER: This family comedy came to television in 1953 as an adaptation of a hit play and best-selling book by Clarence Day. The Day family on television were Leon Ames as Clarence Day, Sr.; Lurene Tuttle as his wife Vinnie; and their sons (standing, left to right) Ralph Reed as Clarence, Jr., Ronald Keith as Whitney, Freddie Leiston as John, and (bottom) Harvey Grant as Harlan.

MAKE ROOM FOR DADDY

appeared on television in 1953 with Danny Thomas starring as Danny Williams, a night-club entertainer who often had to spend long periods of time away from home. Thomas played the leading role with warmth and understanding, since the show's basic premise paralleled his own life. Jean Hagen left the cast in 1957 and was replaced by Marjorie Lord. The show's title was also changed, to *The Danny Thomas Show*.

(Top, right) The first Danny Williams family: Jean Hagen as his wife, Rusty Hamer and Sherry Jackson as his children, Jesse White as his friend and agent, and Danny Thomas as Danny Williams.

(Right) Thomas and Jean Hagen in a scene from an early show in the *Make Room for Daddy* series.

(Below) The second Danny Williams family: Rusty Hamer, Angela Cartwright, Sherry Jackson, Danny Thomas, and Marjorie Lord.

FATHER KNOWS BEST
first appeared on television in 1954. It was the saga of the Anderson family, with Robert Young and Jane Wyatt as parents Jim and Margaret Anderson, and Billy Gray, Elinor Donahue, and Lauren Chapin as children Bud, Betty, and Kathy. Unlike so many other family comedies in which the father was portrayed as a near idiot, *Father Knows Best* showed its leading character as a mature and responsible parent. The program's humor was incidental to its depiction of middle-class American family life. After the show had completed its run, Robert Young returned to television with a program called *Window on Main Street,* which was broadcast for a single season. *Father Knows Best* is currently being rerun on local stations.

(Above) Robert Young celebrates Valentine's Day with a kiss for his youngest daughter, played by Lauren Chapin.

(Right) In this scene of domestic bliss, Young is flanked by his son (Billy Gray) and wife (Jane Wyatt).

(Above) THE STU ERWIN SHOW: Erwin played a mild-mannered high-school principal, with June Collyer as his wife. Earlier this show had been called *The Trouble with Father*; later it was titled *The New Stu Erwin Show*. This series (circa 1953) was one of the first to feature a lovable but bumbling father.

(Above) PRIDE OF THE FAMILY: Paul Hartman was the father, Fay Wray was Momma, and the children were Bobby Hyatt and Natalie Wood in this show, which debuted in 1953. The leading character, Albie Morrison, was, of course, lovable but bumbling.

(Left) THE LIFE OF RILEY: Television's classic lovable bumbler, Chester Riley, was played by William Bendix. Marjorie Reynolds portrayed his wife Peg, and Wesley Morgan was Junior. The program first appeared in 1949, with Jackie Gleason and Rosemary De Camp in the leading roles, and was on for two seasons. Bendix started the new series in 1953, and it remained on the air for five years before going into syndication.

THE GOLDBERGS
made its debut on television in 1949, after having achieved the status of a radio classic. Created and written by Gertrude Berg, it mirrored the trials and joys of a Jewish family in the Bronx. Though the show found both humor and warmth in its ethnic background, its major virtue was its perceptive analysis of individuals and their relationships within the family.

In her best-known pose, Gertrude Berg leans from her window before calling out, "Yoo hoo, Mrs. Bloom!"

(Below) The Goldberg family consisted of (left to right) Robert H. Harris as Jake, Arlene McQuade as Rosalie, Tom Taylor as Sammy, Eli Mintz as Uncle David, and Gertrude Berg as Molly. In another television version of the family, Philip Loeb played Jake, and Larry Robinson was Sammy.

(Above) THE DONNA REED SHOW: A motion-picture actress ("From Here to Eternity"), Miss Reed starred in this extra-wholesome situation comedy from 1958 to 1966.

(Top, right) PLEASE DON'T EAT THE DAISIES: Mark Miller and Patricia Crowley (right) played the parents in the Nash family in this adaptation of Jean Kerr's best seller. The show made its debut in 1965.

(Right) OZZIE AND HARRIET: This family-comedy series arrived in 1952. Its principals were actually members of the same family: Ozzie Nelson, his wife Harriet, and their two sons Ricky and David. Though both remained with the show as they grew older, Ricky and David embarked on show-business careers of their own.

(Below) WONDERFUL JOHN ACTON: The saga of an Irish-American family living in the Ohio River Valley shortly after World War I, the show featured (left to right) Harry Holcombe, Virginia Dwyer, Ronnie Walken, and Ian Martin. It made its debut in 1953.

(Top) NORBY: David Wayne appeared as Pearson Norby and Joan Lorring portrayed his wife Helen in this comedy about a household in Pearl River. The show was first broadcast in 1954.

(Above) THE ALDRICH FAMILY: The television version of the radio series, the show featured (left to right) Bobby Ellis, Barbara Robbins, House Jameson, and June Dayton. It made its first video appearance in 1949. Jameson was a member of the original Aldrich family, which began on radio in 1939.

(Below) DECEMBER BRIDE: In this "family portrait" are Frances Rafferty and Dean Miller in the roles of the daughter and son-in-law; Spring Byington starring as Lily Ruskin; Harry Morgan as Pete, the next-door neighbor; and Verna Felton as Hilda, Lily's friend and comedy accomplice. The program debuted in 1954.

(Above) GUESTWARD HO!: Based on a book about a couple who run an inn in the Southwest, this 1960 show included in its cast Mark Miller, J. Carrol Naish, Joanne Dru, and Earle Hodgins.

(Below) THE HATHAWAYS: The story of a couple who have a house full of monkeys, this program was first telecast in 1961 and starred Peggy Cass and the Marquis Chimps.

(Above) THE ED WYNN SHOW: Wynn played a grandfather, and Sherri Alberoni portrayed his granddaughter, in this 1958 family comedy. □ *(Top, left)* THE WORLD OF MR. SWEENEY: Charles Ruggles was Sweeney and Glenn Walker was his grandson in this series which began in 1953 as a weekly feature on *The Kate Smith Hour.* □ *(Top, right)* LEAVE IT TO BEAVER: The Cleaver family included Hugh Beaumont and Barbara Billingsley as the mother and father, Jerry Mathers as Beaver, and Tony Dow as his older brother Wally. *Beaver,* which made its debut in 1957, was one of the best of the situation comedies because of its sensitivity in both writing and acting. □ *(Second from top, right)* THE DENNIS O'KEEFE SHOW: Hope Emerson and Rickey Kelman were starred with O'Keefe in this 1959 situation comedy. □ *(Right)* ROOM FOR ONE MORE: Timothy Rooney (Mickey's son) played an adopted child and Andrew Duggan was his father in this show, which first appeared in 1962. □ *(Bottom, right)* PECK'S BAD GIRL: Marsha Hunt and Wendell Corey were the parents, with Patty McCormack as their daughter in this 1959 program. □ *(Below)* MY THREE SONS: Fred MacMurray played the widowed father, William Frawley was the grandfather, and the boys (left to right) were Tim Considine, Stanley Livingston, and Don Grady when this long-running series started in 1959.

(Above) GIDGET: Sally Field starred as a surfing teen-ager in this 1965–66 situation comedy. □ *(Top, left)* YOUNG MR. BOBBIN: Jackie Kelk played an eager-beaver young businessman; Jane Seymour (left) and Nydia Westman were his maiden aunts in the 1951 comedy. □ *(Left)* LEAVE IT TO LARRY: Eddie Albert was a befuddled shoe clerk in this 1952 comedy. □ *(Second from bottom, left)* THE MANY LOVES OF DOBIE GILLIS: Dwayne Hickman (as Dobie) is surrounded by some of his many loves in this scene from the Max Shulman comedy series, which was first telecast in 1959. □ *(Bottom, left)* JAMIE: David Susskind produced this series, which featured (left to right) Polly Rowles, Ernest Truex, Brandon deWilde (as Jamie), and Kathy Nolan. The program was first seen in 1954. □ *(Below)* HAPPY: Happy, a baby who could think out loud, was portrayed alternately by twins David and Steven Born. The show made its debut in 1960. □ *(Bottom, right)* THE PATTY DUKE SHOW: Miss Duke played look-alike, teen-age cousins in a series first broadcast in 1963.

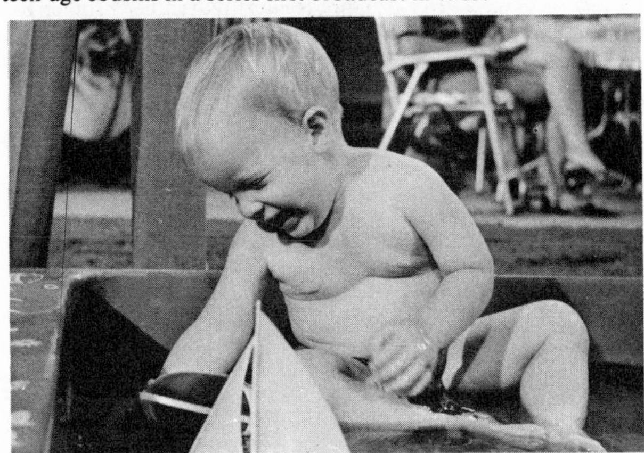

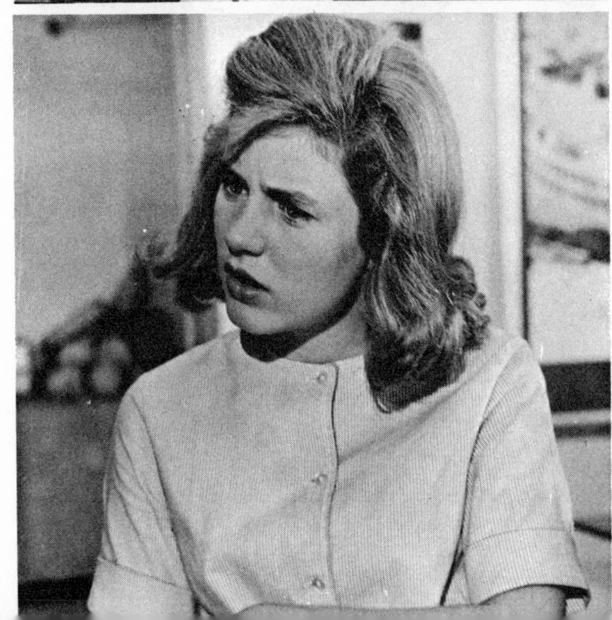

(Above) MY SON JEEP: Anne Sargent provided the romantic interest, Martin Huston (center) was Jeep, and Jeffrey Lynn was Doc Allison, a widower practicing medicine in a small town, in the 1953 series. □ *(Top, right)* KENTUCKY JONES: Dennis Weaver, who limped through *Gunsmoke* for many seasons, was a veterinarian in this 1964 series, which also featured young Rickey Der as a Chinese refugee. □ *(Right)* THE BING CROSBY SHOW: The Old Groaner with Diane Sherry, who played his precocious daughter in a show which premiered in 1964. □ *(Second from bottom, right)* THAT'S MY BOY: This 1954 comedy starred Eddie Mayehoff as ex-football player Jarrin' Jack Jackson and Gil Stratton, Jr. as his bookworm son. □ *(Bottom, right)* BACHELOR FATHER: John Forsythe was the "bachelor father," and Noreen Corcoran played Kelly, his teen-aged niece, in this 1957 series. □ *(Below)* TOO YOUNG TO GO STEADY: Brigid Bazlen was Pam, the fourteen-year-old daughter of a lawyer, in this comedy which arrived in 1959. □ *(Bottom, left)* A DATE WITH JUDY: Mary Linn Beller was Judy, Peter Avramo (center) played her brother Randolph, and Jimmie Sommer was her boyfriend Oogie in a show first seen in 1951.

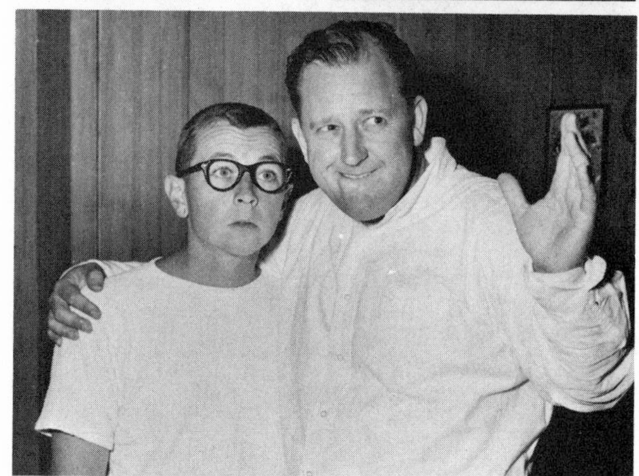

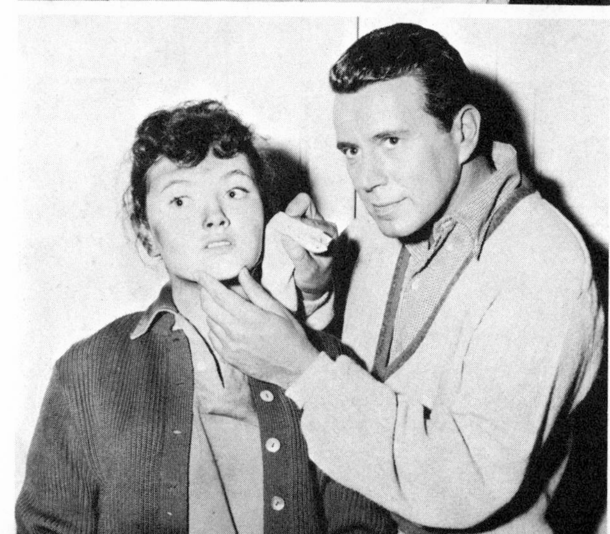

MY FAVORITE HUSBAND: Barry Nelson was starred as George Cooper, and Joan Caulfield portrayed his wife Liz (below) in a series which debuted in 1953. Miss Caulfield was later replaced by Vanessa Brown (above).

(Above) BLONDIE: Arthur Lake was Dagwood and Pamela Britton played Blondie in the television version of the Chic Young comic strip, first broadcast in 1954.

(Top, right) THE BURNS AND ALLEN SHOW: George and Gracie were first seen in this comedy series in 1950. Also featured in the cast were Bea Benaderet and Larry Keating as Blanche and Harry Morton. The show changed its format somewhat in 1958, when Gracie left the series.

(Left) FIBBER MCGEE AND MOLLY: Another adaptation, this one of a famed radio show, starred Bob Sweeney as Fibber and Cathy Lewis as Molly. This version of the series had its premiere in 1959.

(Bottom, left) EASY ACES: In 1949 Goodman Ace and his wife Jane did a video adaptation of the radio favorite.

(Below) HEAVEN FOR BETSY: Jack Lemmon and Cynthia Stone (Mrs. Lemmon at that time) costarred in a twice-a-week domestic comedy in 1952.

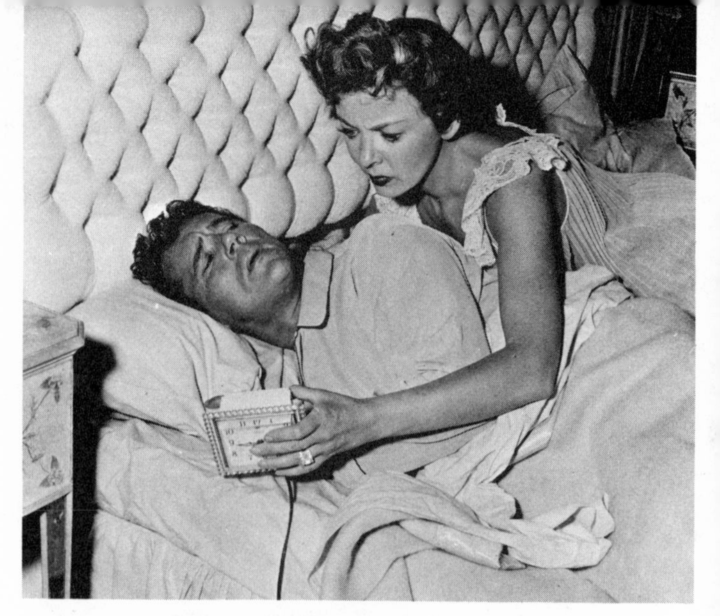

(*Above*) MR. ADAMS AND EVE: Howard Duff and Ida Lupino were a pair of married movie stars in this 1957 situation comedy.

(*Below*) THE RAY BOLGER SHOW: Marjie Millar was Bolger's girl friend in this comedy, which began in 1953 under the title *Where's Raymond?*

(*Bottom*) ETHEL AND ALBERT: Peg Lynch was Ethel and Alan Bunce played Albert in the 1953 series.

(*Top*) THE THIN MAN: In 1957 Phyllis Kirk and Peter Lawford (with their faithful dog, Asta) played the roles made famous in motion pictures by Myrna Loy and William Powell.

(*Above*) LIFE WITH ELIZABETH: Del Moore was Alvin and Betty White was Elizabeth in a syndicated domestic-comedy series. Miss White also starred (in 1957–58) in a series titled *A Date with the Angels*.

(*Below*) JOE AND MABEL: Joe (Larry Blyden) loved Mabel (Nita Talbot) in a comedy which also featured Luella Gear. It debuted in 1956.

(Above) ANGEL: Marshall Thompson and Annie Fargé starred in this 1960 comedy about a young man and his French bride.

(Below) THE MARGE AND GOWER CHAMPION SHOW: Jack Whiting was featured in this 1957 series, which boasted music and dancing as well as comedy.

(Bottom) MARGIE: Cynthia Pepper played the teen-age heroine and Dick Gering was the high-school hero. The show debuted in 1961.

(Top) I MARRIED JOAN: Jim Backus played a judge, and comedienne Joan Davis was his wife in this long-running series first aired in 1952.

(Above) DICK AND THE DUCHESS: Hazel Court was starred in a detective comedy which debuted in 1957. Dick was played by Patrick O'Neal.

(Below) THE CARA WILLIAMS SHOW: Frank Aletter costarred with Cara Williams in a 1964 comedy about a husband and wife who have to keep their marriage a secret.

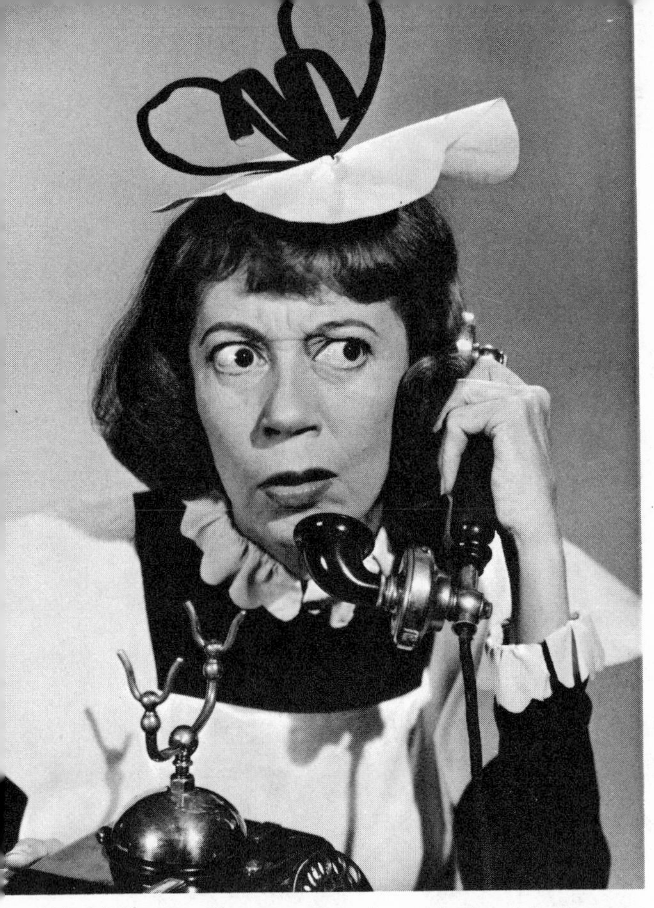

(Above) GRINDL: She was a comedy maid, played by Imogene Coca, in 1963.

(Above) OUR MAN HIGGINS: Stanley Holloway was a butler in this 1962 series.

(Below) HAZEL: In 1961 Shirley Booth debuted in a series about a maid based on the "Saturday Evening Post" cartoons by Ted Key.

(Below) BEULAH: The central role of this comedy series, that of a Negro domestic, was originally played by Ethel Waters in 1950. It was later performed by both Hattie McDaniel and Louise Beavers (below).

Mr. Peepers
was the shy science teacher at Jefferson Junior High, often beleaguered but never outwitted. The series was a gem of quiet, underplayed comedy, and Wally Cox, in the title role, was one of those classic examples of perfect casting. *Mr. Peepers* went on the air in 1952 and continued for three seasons.

(Above) Pat Benoit portrayed the school nurse, Nancy Remington, who wed Peepers a year before the series ended in 1955.

(Top, left) Randall played Harvey Weskit, Peepers' know-it-all faculty colleague.

(Below) The *Mr. Peepers* cast: Wally Cox, Tony Randall, Marion Lorne, and Patricia Benoit.

(Above) OUR MISS BROOKS: Eve Arden was the wisecracking English teacher and Gale Gordon the apoplectic principal in the popular comedy which bowed in 1952.

(Top, right) MRS. G. GOES TO COLLEGE: Gertrude Berg was the mature student and Sir Cedric Hardwicke her instructor in this 1961 situation comedy.

(Bottom, right) HANK: Dick Kallman played Hank in this 1965 comedy about a student who attends college classes even though he is not registered.

(Below) HALLS OF IVY: Ronald Colman starred as Dr. William Todhunter Hall, president of Ivy College, and his wife Benita Hume played Mrs. Hall. The series premiered in 1954.

THE PHIL SILVERS SHOW (originally titled *You'll Never Get Rich*) made its debut in 1955. Silvers was Ernie Bilko, master sergeant and master schemer, who devoted all his waking hours to the pursuit of loose cash. Stationed in Kansas in an obscure army camp which had long been forgotten by the Pentagon brass, Bilko and his buddies conjured up new money-making ventures in each episode. The series, created by Nat Hiken, continued until 1959.

(Above) Bilko with members of his platoon, which included Allan Melvin and Harvey Lembeck (seated on either side of Silvers), Herbie Faye and Billy Sands (both standing, right).

(Top, left) Phil Silvers as the army's greatest con artist.

(Left) Elisabeth Fraser was Bilko's WAC girl friend, and Paul Ford was the always-outfoxed Colonel Hall.

(Below) Maurice Gosfield as Private Doberman, platoon patsy.

(Above) No Time for Sergeants: Based on Mac Hyman's best-selling book and hit play, this story of a good-natured hillbilly dogface starred Sammy Jackson. This series was first broadcast in 1964; some years before, Andy Griffith had been featured in the *U. S. Steel Hour* presentation of the comedy.

(Below) Broadside: Another attempt at service humor, this one featured (left to right) Kathy Nolan, Joan Staley, Lois Roberts, and Sheila James as WAVE mechanics assigned to a South Pacific island during World War II. It debuted in 1964.

(Top) Hennesey: Jackie Cooper played a navy doctor in this 1959 service comedy. Also in the cast were Abby Dalton and Roscoe Karns.

(Above) Mona McCluskey: Denny Miller was an air force sergeant and Juliet Prowse the wife (and Hollywood star) who vows they will live on his service salary. The show was first aired in 1965.

(Below) The Soldiers: Hal March and Tom D'Andrea were the hapless GI's in this series about the humorous side of barracks life, first telecast in 1955.

(Above) MR. ROBERTS: A hit play and a movie, both based on Thomas Heggen's book, preceded this version of life aboard a navy supply ship during World War II. It was first telecast in 1965 and starred Roger Smith (left) in the title role, with Richard Sinatra as D'Angelo.

(Top, left) F TROOP: Larry Storch and Forrest Tucker were cavalrymen, and Edward Everett Horton played an Indian called Roaring Chicken in this slapstick portrayal of army life on the Old Frontier. It debuted in 1965.

(Left) GOMER PYLE, USMC: Another good-natured recruit, this one a marine, is played by Jim Nabors. Nabors was a graduate of the Danny Thomas production complex (he had previously appeared on *The Andy Griffith Show*) when this series began in 1964. He is shown here with Margaret Ann Peterson.

(Bottom, left) MCHALE'S NAVY: Ernest Borgnine's movie roles had seen him cast as a shy butcher ("Marty") and a hissable villain ("From Here to Eternity" and "Bad Day at Black Rock"). In 1962 he tried farce as Commander McHale, skipper of a PT boat with the most lackadaisical crew in the navy. Here, he is flanked by Joe Flynn (left) and Tim Conway.

(Below) HOGAN'S HEROES: A novel twist on service comedies is this one, set in a German POW camp during World War II. When it was first telecast in 1965, it was well received by most critics, although some noted that it was difficult to laugh at any situation involving Nazi prisoners. Featured were Werner Klemperer as Commandant Klink, John Banner as Schultz, and Bob Crane as Hogan.

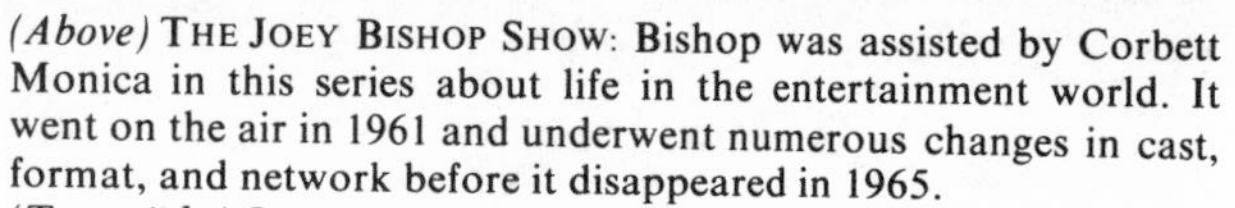

(Above) THE JOEY BISHOP SHOW: Bishop was assisted by Corbett Monica in this series about life in the entertainment world. It went on the air in 1961 and underwent numerous changes in cast, format, and network before it disappeared in 1965.
(Top, right) LOVE AND MARRIAGE: Another comedy about the ups and downs of show biz, this one featured William Demarest (left) as a music publisher and Stubby Kaye as his song-plugger. It debuted in 1959.
(Right) SO THIS IS HOLLYWOOD: Virginia Gibson (bottom), Jimmy Lydon, and Mitzi Green were featured in a 1954 series about two girls trying to make good in Movietown.
(Bottom, right) HARRY'S GIRLS: Larry Blyden was Harry, manager of a troupe of show girls on a tour of European nightclubs. It was telecast in 1963.
(Below) IT'S ALWAYS JAN: Janis Paige starred as a nightclub singer in this 1956 show.

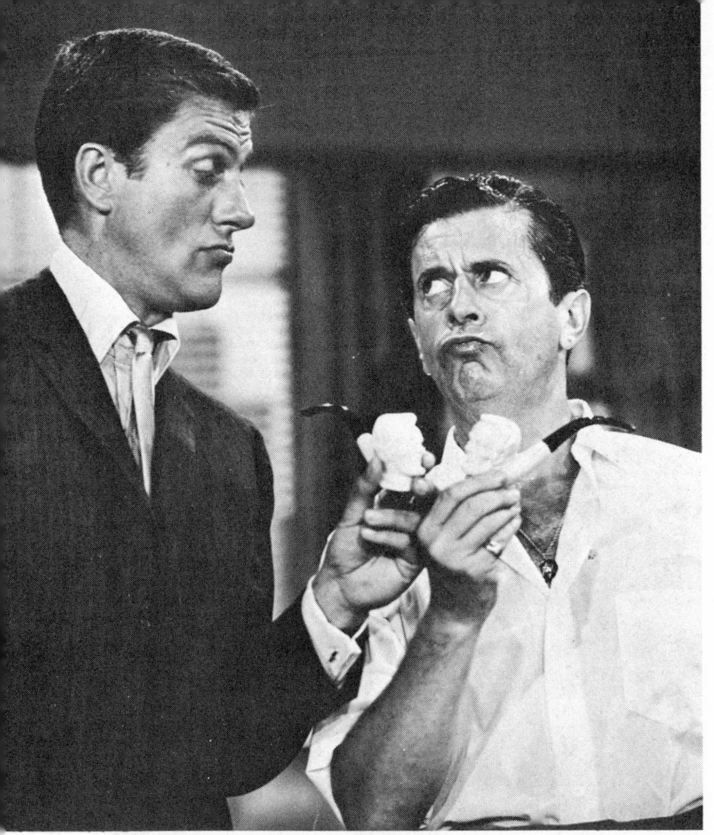

(Above) Buddy (Morey Amsterdam) and Rob (Dick Van Dyke) compare pipes in this early (1962) episode of the show.

THE DICK VAN DYKE SHOW
was first shown in 1961 and continued on the air through the 1966 season. It starred Dick Van Dyke as comedy writer Rob Petrie; Mary Tyler Moore as his wife Laura; Morey Amsterdam and Rose Marie as Buddy and Sally, the other two members of the writing team; Richard Deacon as Mel, the producer; and, occasionally, Carl Reiner as Alan Brady, the tyrannical star of a mythical television show. Reiner also wrote and directed some episodes, and ex-movie heavy Sheldon Leonard supervised the production of the series. *The Dick Van Dyke Show* got off to a slow start in the ratings race and faced cancellation, but it won a reprieve from its sponsor and went on to become one of the most popular and successful shows on the air. Usually well-written, and always well-played, the series differed from many of its contemporaries in the situation-comedy field in that it was often genuinely funny.

(Below) Rob and Laura (Mary Tyler Moore) re-create an incident from Rob's army days in this 1964 scene.

(Below) The cast: (top, left to right) Richard Deacon, Rose Marie, Morey Amsterdam; (bottom) Mary Tyler Moore, Dick Van Dyke.

(Above) BEWITCHED: Agnes Moorehead (left) is Endora, and Elizabeth Montgomery her daughter Samantha, television's prettiest witch, in the series which first appeared in 1964. Also featured in the cast: Dick York and the late Alice Pearce.

(Top, right) MY FAVORITE MARTIAN: Ray Walston (left) was the Martian and Bill Bixby was Tim O'Hara in this 1963 fable of a visitor from another planet.

(Right) THE MUNSTERS: 1964 was the year for comedy monsters, and prominent among them was a family of creeps called the Munsters, Fred Gwynne (shown here with Paul Lynde) was Herman, Yvonne DeCarlo was his wife Lily, and Al Lewis was Grandpa.

(Bottom, right) THE ADDAMS FAMILY: Another spooky clan to emerge in 1964 were the video versions of Charles Addams' cartoon creatures. Carolyn Jones (shown) played Morticia, John Astin was Gomez, Jackie Coogan was Uncle Fester, and Ted Cassidy was Lurch.

(Below) I DREAM OF JEANNIE: Barbara Eden played a genie in this 1965 comedy, which also starred Larry Hagman and Hayden Rorke.

(Above) MY MOTHER, THE CAR: A car that talked! Jerry Van Dyke (Dick's brother) was the owner of the car in this 1965 series; Ann Sothern supplied Mother's voice.

(Left) MY LIVING DOLL: Julie Newmar was a robot named Rhoda (here, with guest Michael Jackson), which startled those who visualized robots as more clanky and less cuddly. Robert Cummings costarred in this series, which debuted in 1964.

(Bottom, left) MISTER ED: A horse that talked! This was the premise of the 1961 comedy which starred Alan Young, Connie Hines, and a horse named Ed.

(Below) TOPPER: Leo G. Carroll played Cosmo Topper, Anne Jeffreys and Robert Sterling the charming ghosts in this adaptation of the Thorne Smith novels. The show debuted in 1953 and was the forerunner of the many spirits and nonhumans who materialized on television in the middle sixties.

MICKEY: A swank California motel was the scene of the action in this 1964 series. Mickey Rooney was a Midwesterner who had inherited the place and all the comic difficulties that went with it.

IT'S A MAN'S WORLD: A houseboat was the setting for this imaginative 1963 comedy. In the cast were Glenn Corbett (left), Jan Norris, and Randy Boone.

GILLIGAN'S ISLAND: An exotic island is the setting for this series, which debuted in 1964. Stranded there was Gilligan (Bob Denver), shown here with Mary Foran. When this show came on the air it was almost unanimously condemned by the critics, who attacked it with unparalleled ferocity. Viewers, however, seem to feel differently, and *Gilligan* has scored consistently well in the ratings.

(Above) DUFFY'S TAVERN: "Where the elite meet to eat," manager Archie (Ed Gardner) used to say. First telecast in 1954, *Duffy's* also featured (above) Pattee Chapman as Miss Duffy and Alan Reed as Charlie the waiter. □ *(Top)* THE CHARLIE FARRELL SHOW: The locale for this one, first broadcast in 1956, was the Racquet Club in Palm Springs. Ann Lee (left) and Marie Windsor aided Farrell. □ *(Below)* STUDS' PLACE: This Chicago-based show won loyal support from local fans, then went on the network in 1950. It took place in a restaurant, and featured (left to right) Win Stracke, Studs Terkel, Beverly Younger, and Chet Roble. □ *(Bottom)* CAMP RUNAMUCK: A children's summer camp was the backdrop for this 1965 situation comedy. Some of the grownups were (left to right) Nina Wayne, Arch Johnson, Alice Nunn, and Dave Ketchum.

(Above) STANLEY: Buddy Hackett was Stanley, the manager of a newsstand in a hotel lobby, and Carol Burnett played his girl friend. Max Liebman *(Your Show of Shows)* produced it, but it ran for only one year after its 1956 debut.
(Top, left) BOB CUMMINGS SHOW: The featured role was that of a commercial photographer (Cummings) who always seemed to be surrounded by a horde of beautiful girls. One of them (right) was Joi Lansing. This series was first seen in 1955, and Cummings used the same formula in several subsequent television comedies.
(Left) DOC CORKLE: Eddie Mayehoff was a dentist and Connie Marshall was his daughter in this 1952 comedy. Not shown, but also featured in the cast, were Arnold Stang, Hope Emerson, Billie Burke, and Chester Conklin.
(Bottom, left) THE PEOPLE'S CHOICE: Jackie Cooper was the mayor of a small town in this 1955 series which featured a basset hound named Cleo.
(Below) DEAR PHOEBE: Another 1955 comedy, this one costarred Peter Lawford and Marcia Henderson as colleagues on a newspaper staff.

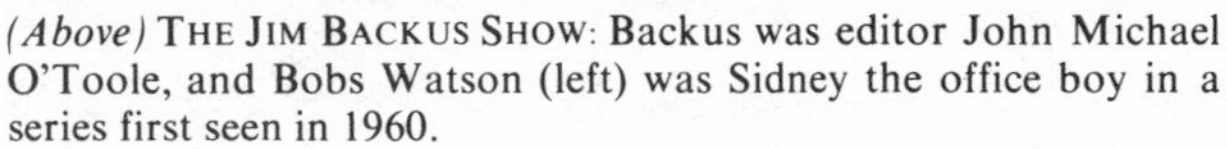

(Above) THE JIM BACKUS SHOW: Backus was editor John Michael O'Toole, and Bobs Watson (left) was Sidney the office boy in a series first seen in 1960.
(Top, right) THE TYCOON: Walter Brennan was a wheeler-dealer and Van Williams played his aide. The show premiered in 1964.
(Right) THE DUKE: Paul Gilbert was a retired prizefighter with a penchant for the arts in this 1954 series.
(Bottom, right) ICHABOD AND ME: Robert Sterling (left) played a small-town newspaper editor. He is shown here with writer Rod Serling, who turned performer for this episode in the series. It went on the air in 1962.
(Below) THE RAY MILLAND SHOW: This one took place on a college campus. Shown with Milland is guest star Miriam Hopkins. An earlier version of this 1955 show was entitled *Meet Mr. McNutley*, then *Meet Mr. McNulty*.

(Top) I'M DICKENS . . . HE'S FENSTER: John Astin was Dickens and Marty Ingels (shown) was Fenster in a 1962 series about two not-so-handymen.

(Above) THE MICKEY ROONEY SHOW: Rooney was "the irrepressible Mickey Mulligan" in this 1954 show.

(Below) THE ADVENTURES OF HIRAM HOLLIDAY: In 1956 Wally Cox returned to television in the unlikely role of an international adventurer. He is shown here with Angela Greene.

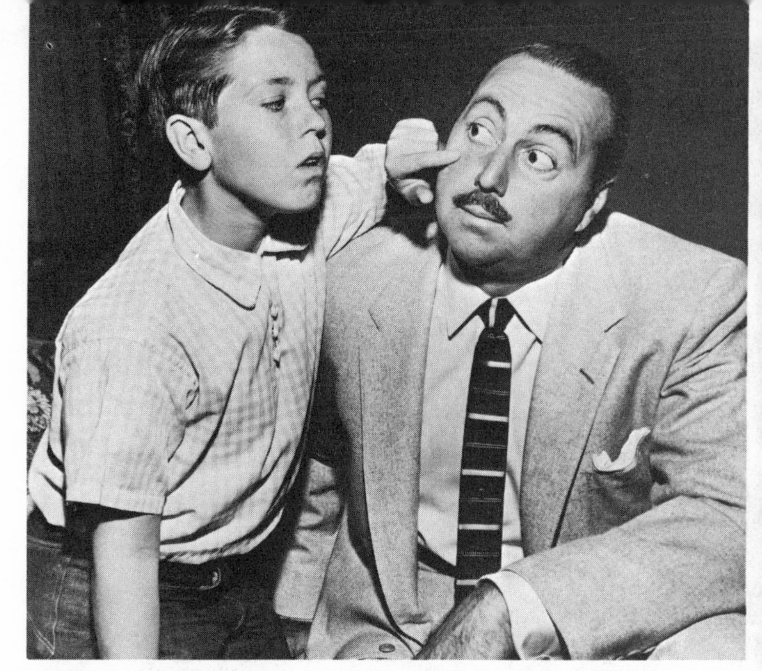

(Above) THE GREAT GILDERSLEEVE: In this 1955 adaptation of a popular radio program, Gildy was played by Willard Waterman and his nephew Leroy was enacted by Ronald Keith.

(Below) IT'S A GREAT LIFE: A comedy of domestic strife, it featured (left to right) James Dunn, William Bishop, and Michael O'Shea. It was first seen in 1954.

(Bottom) HARRIGAN & SON: Father and son were law partners in a comedy courtroom series first seen in 1960. Harrigan, Sr. was Pat O'Brien (left); Junior was Roger Perry.

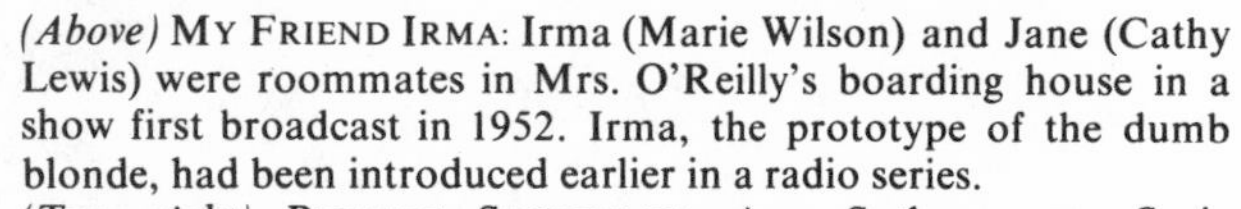

(Above) My Friend Irma: Irma (Marie Wilson) and Jane (Cathy Lewis) were roommates in Mrs. O'Reilly's boarding house in a show first broadcast in 1952. Irma, the prototype of the dumb blonde, had been introduced earlier in a radio series.
(Top, right) Private Secretary: Ann Sothern was Susie McNamara, secretary to a theatrical agent. The show was first telecast in 1954.
(Right) Those Whiting Girls: Margaret (left) and Barbara Whiting costarred in the 1955 series in which they played themselves.
(Bottom, right) Willy: June Havoc played a lawyer in this situation comedy which appeared in 1954.
(Below) Oh! Susanna: Gale Storm (right) was Susanna, the social director on a luxury liner, in this 1956 production which was but one of several Gale Storm comedy series. Her sidekick in the *Oh! Susanna* series was ZaSu Pitts.

(Above) HONESTLY, CELESTE!: Celeste Holm starred as a small-town girl working on a big-town newspaper in this 1954 comedy.

(Top, left) SALLY: Joan Caulfield and Johnny Desmond were the costars of this series, first seen in 1957. Marion Lorne was also in the cast.

(Left) GLYNIS: Glynis Johns (shown here trying to revive Eddie Foy, Jr.) was a writer of mystery stories in this 1963 spoof. Keith Andes was her private-eye husband.

(Below) HOW TO MARRY A MILLIONAIRE: The three man-hunting females in this 1958 comedy series were (left to right) Barbara Eden, Merry Anders, and Lori Nelson.

(Above) THE FARMER'S DAUGHTER: Inger Stevens had the starring role as the Swedish farm girl who marries a Congressman. The program premiered in 1963.
(Top, right) MEET MILLIE: In this 1952 comedy Elena Verdugo starred as a typical Manhattan secretary, while Ross Ford played the boss's son. Florence Halop was featured as Millie's mother.
(Right) LOVE THAT JILL: Anne Jeffreys and Robert Sterling were rival owners of model agencies in this 1958 show.
(Below) TUGBOAT ANNIE: Minerva Urecal was the skipper of the tugboat Narcissus in this syndicated 1958 series. The show was based on the movie of the same name, which had starred Marie Dressler.

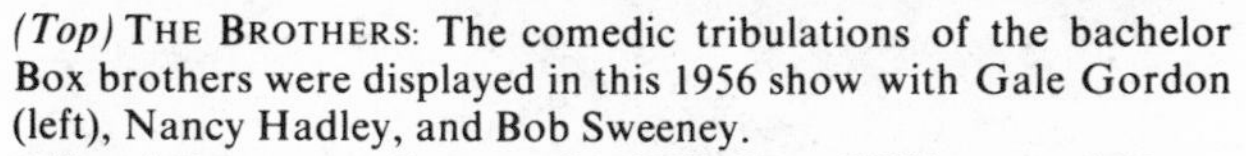

(Top) THE BROTHERS: The comedic tribulations of the bachelor Box brothers were displayed in this 1956 show with Gale Gordon (left), Nancy Hadley, and Bob Sweeney.

(Above) PETE AND GLADYS: In 1960 Cara Williams and Harry Morgan teamed up in this comedy of love and marriage, an offshoot of *December Bride*. They are shown above with Bill Hinnant (right).

(Below) THE JOHN FORSYTHE SHOW: Forsythe, surrounded by Ann B. Davis (left) and Elsa Lanchester, was an ex-air force officer who inherited a girl's school in this 1965 series.

(Above) HEY, JEANNIE!: Jeannie Carson played a Scottish miss just off the boat and caught up in the excitement and adventure of the big city. Her friend the cabbie was Allen Jenkins. The program premiered in 1956.

(Below) OH, THOSE BELLS!: This 1962 slapstick series starred the Wiere Brothers as custodians of props in a theatrical warehouse. Pictured below are Herbert (left) and Harry Wiere. Missing: Sylvester.

(Bottom) MANY HAPPY RETURNS: John McGiver (right) was joined by Russell Collins (left) and Mickey Manners in a 1964 entry about the complaint bureau of a department store.

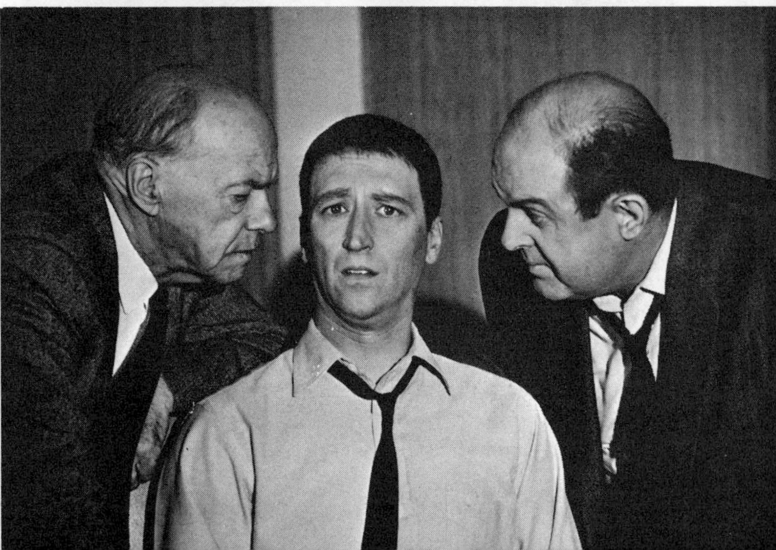

(*Above*) LIFE WITH LUIGI: J. Carrol Naish (left) was the newly arrived immigrant who settles in Chicago; Alan Reed was Pasquale, the friend who was forever trying to make a match between his sister Rosa and Luigi. This early series was first shown in 1948. Naish, a versatile character actor, later employed other accents when he was seen as Charlie Chan and as an Indian in *Guestward Ho!*

(*Below*) BONINO: Ezio Pinza had the leading role in this story of a retired concert singer who was the father of a large family of motherless children. Mary Wickes played Martha, the family maid. The show debuted in 1953.

(*Above*) THE REAL McCOYS: This long-running hillbilly comedy was first shown in 1957. Walter Brennan was Grampa, and Richard Crenna (right) was Luke.

(*Below*) AMOS 'N' ANDY: This was the show that became an American fixation in the dear, departed days of radio. In the television version, which first appeared in 1951, Alvin Childress (left) was Amos, Tim Moore (center) was the Kingfish, and Spencer Williams was Andy. In 1966 CBS withdrew the program from syndication and overseas sale after several civil-rights groups protested that it was a distorted portrayal of Negro life in the United States.

THE BEVERLY HILLBILLIES:
In 1962 CBS first presented this simple comedy of simple country folk who strike it rich and move into posh digs in exclusive Beverly Hills. The reaction was simply incredible. The show was an overnight sensation and quickly moved to a position high in the ratings, a status it was to maintain for several years. During that same period, those critics who were gloomiest about the state of television invariably cited *The Beverly Hillbillies* as the most flagrant example of the decadence of television comedy. Created and produced by Paul Henning, it was based on a time-honored theme: the innocent bumpkins who outwit and confound the city slickers at every turn. It starred Irene Ryan as Granny Clampett (left), Buddy Ebsen as Jed, and Donna Douglas as Elly May. Another member of the Clampett tribe (not shown) was Max Baer, son of the former heavyweight champ.

(Above) THE ANDY GRIFFITH SHOW: Andy was the sheriff of Mayberry, and Don Knotts played his deputy when this comedy series got going in 1960.

(Top, left) CAR 54, WHERE ARE YOU? Fred Gwynne (left) and Joe E. Ross were the minions of the law in this 1962 Nat Hiken concoction.

(Left) COL. FLACK: Humphrey Flack (Alan Mowbray, right) was an amiable con man with a heart of gold. His trusted aide, Frank Jenks, assisted him in fleecing the unwary. The show was first broadcast in 1953.

GET SMART!:
International agents a la James Bond ran rampant through the mid-sixties, but in 1965 a countermovement appeared—and the spy spoofs were upon us. The ultimate in this area of spoofery was *Get Smart!,* which starred Don Adams as Maxwell Smart, the most inefficient secret agent in Christendom. Smart always got his man (with the assistance of Agent 99, Barbara Feldon), by making the most of his chief assets—stupidity and incompetence. Adams had previously appeared as a house detective on *The Bill Dana Show;* Miss Feldon first attracted attention when she was seen in a series of commercials in which she reclined on a tigerskin rug. Shortly after the show went on the air, two of Smart's catch phrases were being repeated endlessly: "Sorry about that, Chief" and "Would you believe. . .?"

They Called Them Spectaculars

UNTIL 1954 "spectacular" was a perfectly respectable adjective. In that year, however, it was transformed into a noun and put to use to identify a new television phenomenon—the lavish extravaganza which began, with increasing frequency, to appear all over the television schedule in place of regularly scheduled programs.

Previously there had been isolated instances of big, one-time-only shows muscling in on the regular schedule. But in 1954 these special shows began arriving by the carload. Sylvester L. Weaver, NBC's president during that period, introduced the spectaculars. His genius for dreaming up new programming concepts was exceeded only by his talent for making them seem immensely exciting. Occasionally they lived up to expectations; more often they did not. But they broke up the monotony of television's rigidly constructed schedules, gave viewers something to stay home for, and every now and then provided a thrilling or joyous moment that made owning a television set more than worthwhile.

It was Weaver's idea to call them spectaculars, and the name caught on everywhere except at the other networks, which did not want to be caught using a term NBC had invented. Eventually NBC dropped it too, when it switched its publicity emphasis from the grandeur of its shows to the fact that increasing numbers

CHAPTER V

of them were being telecast in color as the fifties progressed.

Whatever you choose to call them—and "specials" has become the generally accepted term—all three networks have presented them, and they have been the source of a great many of television's most unforgettable moments: Mary Martin and Ethel Merman singing their duet . . . Fred Astaire dancing . . . Peter Pan flying . . . "Annie Get Your Gun," "Wonderful Town," and "Kiss Me, Kate" coming to television from Broadway . . . Barbra Streisand running wild in a department store . . . Elizabeth Taylor wandering around London . . . Julie Andrews and Carol Burnett having a ball . . . Harry Belafonte, Victor Borge, Gene Kelly, Leontyne Price, Rudolph Nureyev, Art Carney—just about everybody in the world who can sing, dance, or make people laugh has turned up in television's specials. (So have many of the world's greatest plays and actors, but these will be considered in a later chapter.)

In recent years the networks have shied away from specials. Production costs have mounted to stratospheric heights. The ratings race has intensified to the point that the networks are afraid to risk the loss of Nielsen points by preempting sure-thing weekly programs. And many of the men who were responsible for the great specials have drifted away to the movies or the stage.

Still, specials will always be with us. They are the shows which add that extra dimension of surprise, of excitement, and, now and then, of true distinction to the experience of watching television.

And sometimes they are *genuinely* spectacular.

AMAHL AND THE NIGHT VISITORS: On Christmas Eve, 1951, an opera arrived, commissioned specifically for television, which was to become an annual television tradition. Gian Carlo Menotti's "Amahl and the Night Visitors," performed by the NBC Opera Company and produced by Samuel Chotzinoff, has been telecast every year at Christmastime (and once at Easter). In 1951 the crippled shepherd boy, Amahl, was played by Chet Allen. The next year, and for several years thereafter, Bill McIver was Amahl. He is pictured here with Rosemary Kuhlmann as his mother. Miss Kuhlmann originated the role and continued to play it in various new productions of the opera.

(Bottom, right) IRVING BERLIN'S SALUTE TO AMERICA: In a 1951 entertainment special, songwriter Berlin was joined by Tony Martin (at piano), Dinah Shore, and Margaret Truman.

(Below) OLYMPICS TELETHON: Bob Hope and Bing Crosby were the anchor men for a mammoth telethon which raised money for the 1952 U.S. Olympic team.

FORD 50TH ANNIVERSARY SHOW:
On June 15, 1953, Mary Martin and Ethel Merman sang a duet which proved to be one of television's most memorable events—and a turning point in the history of television specials. The show was a lavish anniversary celebration produced by Leland Hayward and telecast simultaneously on CBS and NBC. Marian Anderson, Amos 'n' Andy, Oscar Hammerstein 2nd, Howard Lindsay, Dorothy Stickney, Edward R. Murrow, and Ollie Dragon also performed in the two-hour program, but Merman and Martin stole the show when they sat on two swiveling stools, on a bare stage, and belted out a song medley in their own captivating styles. Since then countless performers have sat on stools on bare television sets and tried to duplicate the excitement of that moment. On that night in 1953 the television special came into its own.

SATINS AND SPURS:
In 1954 the "spectacular" was born—sired and named by Pat Weaver of NBC, and produced by Max Liebman. The first spectacular, on September 12, 1954, was preceded by an extravagant publicity buildup. No program could have lived up to all that ballyhoo, but the ninety-minute musical comedy "Satins and Spurs" did not even come close. Reactions of critics and viewers were so hostile that Betty Hutton, who had made her television debut in the show, decided to retire from show business (though she soon changed her mind). Her role was that of a rodeo queen who falls in love with a magazine reporter (Kevin McCarthy). Despite their disastrous beginning, spectaculars were here to stay.

(Above) BABES IN TOYLAND: Victor Herbert's operetta became Max Liebman's Christmas spectacular in both 1954 and 1955. Jack E. Leonard and Wally Cox were in it, along with Dennis Day and Dave Garroway.

(Below) ONCE UPON AN EASTERTIME: Easter specials of all sorts—some religious, some purely entertaining—sprout every spring. This was one of 1954's, with Gwen Verdon, Bobby Clark, and Doretta Morrow.

(Above) A CHRISTMAS CAROL: *Shower of Stars,* which displaced *Climax!* once a month, presented a musical version of Dickens' story in 1954, with Fredric March as Scrooge. Maxwell Anderson wrote the libretto.

(Below) GENERAL FOODS 25TH ANNIVERSARY SHOW: General Foods adopted Ford's formula (as a number of other companies have done since) and celebrated its anniversary on television in 1954. Rodgers and Hammerstein show tunes were performed by Yul Brynner and Patricia Morison (here doing a scene from "The King and I"), and Mary Martin, Ezio Pinza, Celeste Holm, Gordon MacRae, Tony Martin, Rosemary Clooney, and others.

OPPOSITE PAGE:
(Top, left) OUR TOWN: Thornton Wilder's play was set to music by Sammy Cahn and James Van Heusen for *Producers' Showcase* in 1955. Eva Marie Saint and Paul Newman had the romantic leads, but most of the singing ("Love and Marriage," etc.) was done by Frank Sinatra, as the "Stage Manager."
(Center, left) MADAM BUTTERFLY: Operas have been produced only rarely on television, most often by the NBC Opera Company. Elaine Malbin sang the lead role in this English-language version of Puccini's opera in 1955.
(Bottom, left) THE SLEEPING BEAUTY: Full-length ballets are also television rarities. In 1955 *Producers' Showcase* imported the Sadler's Wells Ballet for a ninety-minute production starring Margot Fonteyn and Michael Somes.
(Top, right) HEIDI: Jeannie Carson starred (with Wally Cox, Elsa Lanchester, and Natalie Wood) in this 1955 musical.
(Center, right) ONE TOUCH OF VENUS: Janet Blair and Russell Nype played in the Ogden Nash-S.J. Perelman-Kurt Weill musical in 1955.
(Bottom, right) GOOD TIMES: This was 1955's first spectacular. Dick Shawn, Judy Holliday, and Steve Allen are shown here during rehearsals.

PETER PAN:
Most spectacular of all the 1955 spectaculars was this gay musical version of Barrie's fantasy. *Producers' Showcase* and Jerome Robbins transferred it from the stage to television on March 7, 1955, and it has been repeated approximately every two years since, with Mary Martin flying high (on wires) as Peter, and Cyril Ritchard getting his just deserts as Captain Hook. Its appearance is always eagerly awaited and joyously welcomed and will continue to be as long as there are children who believe in fairies and adults who relish superior entertainment.

(Above) THE MUSIC OF GERSHWIN: Cab Calloway was united with Ethel Merman, Alfred Drake, Tony Bennett, Eugene List, and Tanaquil LeClercq in this *Max Liebman Presents* show. □ *(Below)* MAURICE CHEVALIER: He was the star of a 1956 *Sunday Spectacular* and has shown up frequently on television through the years. □ *(Bottom)* BLOOMER GIRL: Evalina was played by Barbara Cook on *Producers' Showcase*.

(Top) THE MAGIC FLUTE: Musical specials were flourishing in 1956. The NBC Opera Company presented this one, with Leontyne Price, William Lewis, and John Reardon. □ *(Above)* HIGH TOR: A twenty-year-old stage performer made her first television appearance on March 10, 1956, in *Ford Star Jubilee's* "High Tor"—Julie Andrews (left) appeared with Bing Crosby and Nancy Olson in the musical fantasy based on Maxwell Anderson's play. □ *(Below)* MARCO POLO: Doretta Morrow, Alfred Drake, and Beatrice Kraft were in this original musical coauthored by Neil Simon.

(Above) Victor Borge: Almost every season since 1956 has boasted at least one Borge special.

(Left) The Bachelor: Original musical comedies kept turning up during the mid-fifties—in this one Carol Haney and Jayne Mansfield chased Hal March. Music and lyrics were by Steve Allen.

(Bottom, left) The Lord Don't Play Favorites: This musical had a circus setting and a cast which included Buster Keaton and Kay Starr, plus Robert Stack, Dick Haymes, and Louis Armstrong.

(Below) High Button Shoes: From Broadway came this 1956 *Saturday Spectacular*. Nanette Fabray played opposite Hal March and Don Ameche.

(Above) THE WIZARD OF OZ: CBS bought the television rights to this MGM classic before the prices of such movies became prohibitive (and before movies became a major form of prime-time programming). The network's first showing of "The Wizard of Oz" (1956) was a tremendous success, and the film has been rerun every year since then, during the Christmas season. In this scene Dorothy (Judy Garland) meets the Scarecrow (Ray Bolger) on the Yellow Brick Road.

(Right) HOLIDAY ON ICE: This *Saturday Spectacular* starred Sonja Henie.

(Bottom, right) JACK AND THE BEANSTALK: Joel Gray was Jack and Billy Gilbert was Mr. Poopledoop in this *Producers' Showcase* special. Others in the cast were Celeste Holm, Cyril Ritchard, Peggy King, Dennis King, and Arnold Stang.

(Below) THE STINGIEST MAN IN TOWN: Nearly every Christmas season brings a new treatment of Dickens' "A Christmas Carol." In 1956 Basil Rathbone tried his first singing role, as Scrooge. Martyn Green was Bob Cratchit in this ninety-minute holiday special produced for *The Alcoa Hour*.

CINDERELLA:
A 1957 highlight was this ninety-minute Rodgers and Hammerstein musical, written expressly for television and emanating live from a lavishly appointed New York studio. Julie Andrews (shown here with Oscar Hammerstein 2nd, left, and Richard Rodgers) portrayed Cinderella. Jon Cypher was her prince, and the cast also included Howard Lindsay, Dorothy Stickney, Ilka Chase, Kaye Ballard, Alice Ghostley, Edith Adams, and, as one of twenty dancers in the production numbers, Joe Layton—who a few years later would stage and choreograph some outstanding television specials. Ralph Nelson directed. In 1965 a new version, with Leslie Ann Warren as Cinderella, was telecast and taped for reshowing in later years.

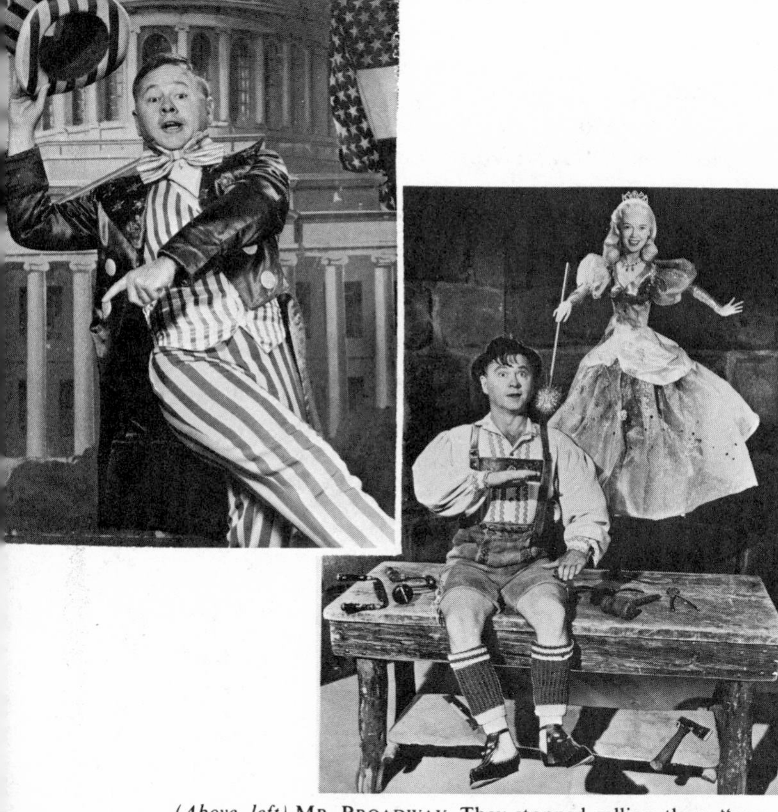

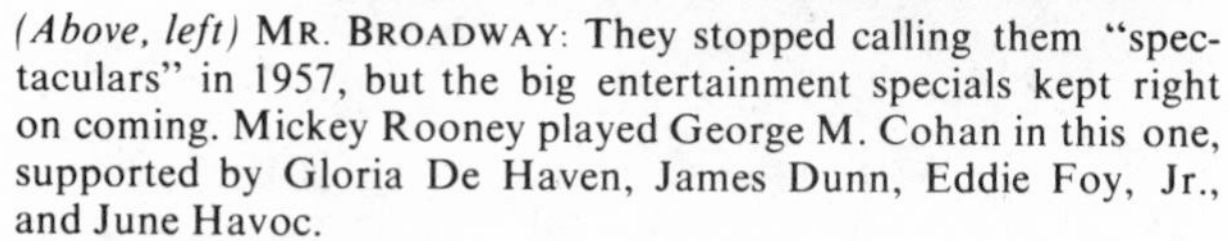

(Above, left) MR. BROADWAY: They stopped calling them "spectaculars" in 1957, but the big entertainment specials kept right on coming. Mickey Rooney played George M. Cohan in this one, supported by Gloria De Haven, James Dunn, Eddie Foy, Jr., and June Havoc.

(Above, center) PINOCCHIO: Six months later Rooney was back in another musical, as Pinocchio. Fran Allison was his guardian angel. The show was broadcast on radio as well as television.

(Above, right) RUGGLES OF RED GAP: Peter Lawford, Imogene Coca, and Jane Powell were in this one.

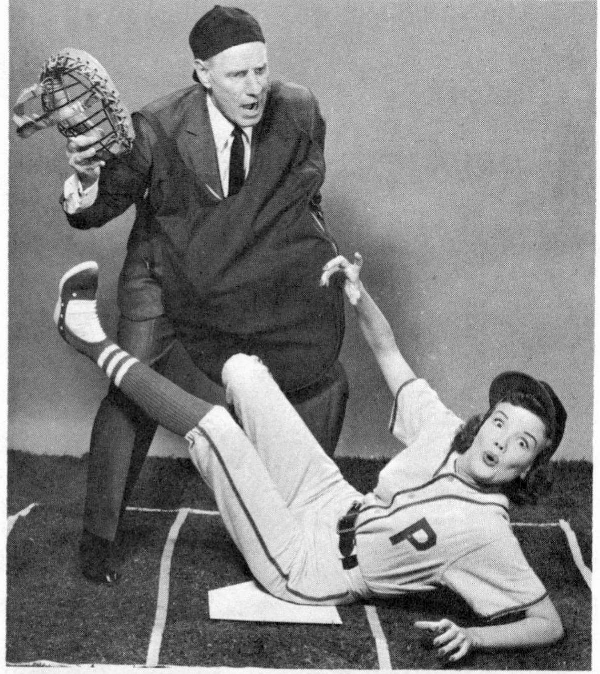

(Right) A MAN'S GAME: *Kaiser Aluminum Hour* observed the coming of the 1957 baseball season by hiring Leo Durocher and Nanette Fabray to do an original musical.

(Bottom, right) FESTIVAL OF MAGIC: Milbourne Christopher was one of several magicians in this *Producers' Showcase* special. Here Christopher works with model Eva Lynd. Ernie Kovacs was the show's host.

(Below) THE YEOMEN OF THE GUARD: A captivating version of the Gilbert and Sullivan operetta was offered by *Hallmark Hall of Fame,* with Alfred Drake, Celeste Holm, Bill Hayes, and Barbara Cook singing the lead roles.

(*Below*) MIKE TODD'S PARTY: The fiasco of the 1957 season was this "little party for a few chums" which Mike Todd tossed in Madison Square Garden to celebrate the first birthday of his movie "Around the World in 80 Days." Many celebrities were invited to the black-tie affair, but most had the good sense to stay home and watch the debacle on television. A few showed up—Georgie Jessel, V. K. Krishna Menon, Elizabeth Taylor (Todd's wife), Sir Cedric Hardwicke (who barely managed to keep from falling off an elephant), among others. But the Garden was packed with eighteen thousand freeloaders who turned into a mutinous mob after some chiseling vendors started charging extortionate prices for hot dogs and domestic champagne which were supposed to be free. Todd smiled happily throughout the entire shambles, very little of which was captured by the television cameras.

(*Above*) ANNIE GET YOUR GUN: Irving Berlin's Broadway musical became a two-hour television special in 1957, with Mary Martin as Annie Oakley, John Raitt as Frank Butler, and William O'Neal as Buffalo Bill Cody. Vincent J. Donehue directed.

(*Top, left*) THE PIED PIPER OF HAMELIN: Van Johnson starred with Claude Rains, Kay Starr, and Doodles Weaver.

(*Below*) THE STANDARD OIL COMPANY (NEW JERSEY) 75TH ANNIVERSARY SHOW: This one had the longest title of 1957 and one of the largest casts, as dozens of stars were on hand for the celebration. Eddie Mayehoff, Brandon deWilde, and Bert Lahr were three of them. The host was Kirk Douglas.

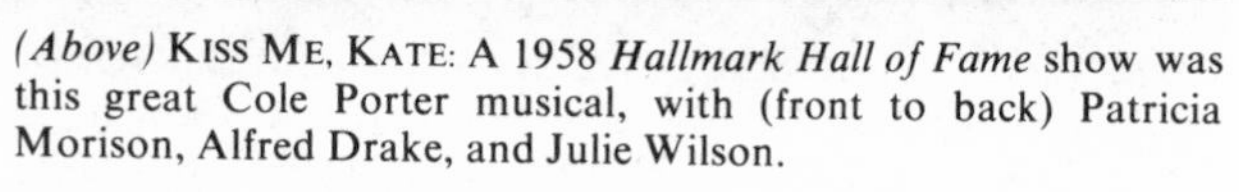

(Above) KISS ME, KATE: A 1958 *Hallmark Hall of Fame* show was this great Cole Porter musical, with (front to back) Patricia Morison, Alfred Drake, and Julie Wilson.

(Top, right) THE RED MILL: This *Du Pont Show of the Month* featured Evelyn Rudie, Shirley Jones, and Donald O'Connor, plus Nichols and May, and Harpo Marx.

(Right) HANS BRINKER OR THE SILVER SKATES: Another 1958 *Hallmark Hall of Fame* adaptation was this children's classic, starring Dick Button, Peggy King, and Tab Hunter.

(Below) HANSEL AND GRETEL: Red Buttons was Hansel (Barbara Cook, Gretel).

(Above) WONDERFUL TOWN: Another big stage musical was transferred to television in 1958, with Rosalind Russell, Jacquelyn McKeever, and Sydney Chaplin singing the Bernstein-Comden-Green score. □ *(Below, left)* THE NUTCRACKER: For its 1958 Christmas Night show *Playhouse 90* presented this Tchaikovsky-Balanchine ballet, danced by Edward Villella and other members of the New York City Ballet. Several different versions of "The Nutcracker" have subsequently been televised. □ *(Below, right)* ART CARNEY MEETS PETER AND THE WOLF: Carney and the Bil and Cora Baird Marionettes were the cast of this special, with music by Prokofiev, lyrics by Ogden Nash.

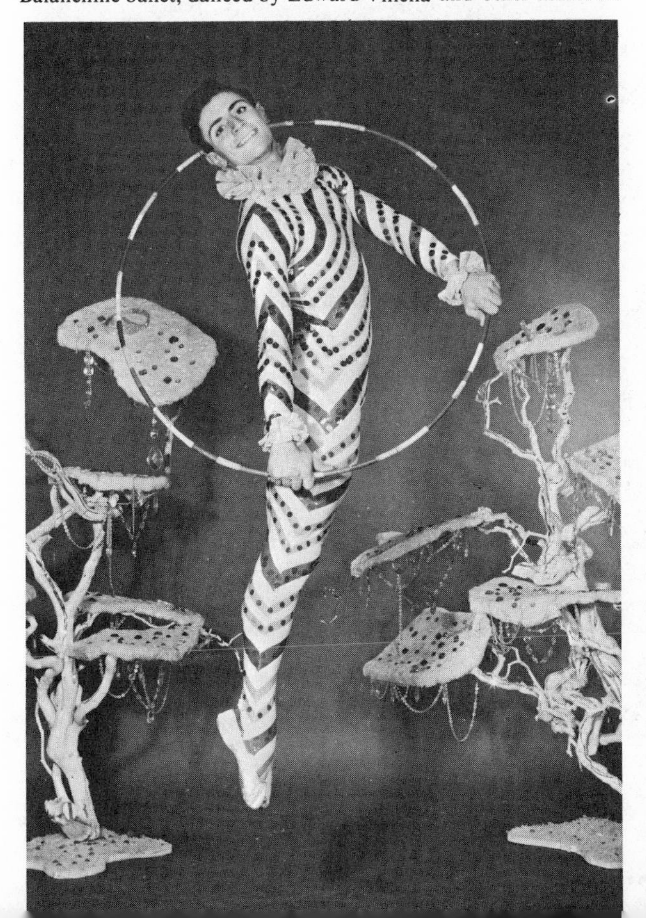

AN EVENING WITH FRED ASTAIRE:
This turned out to be the biggest television event of 1958. Astaire combined with Barrie Chase, the Jonah Jones Quartet, producer Bud Yorkin, and choreographer Hermes Pan for an hour of dancing (and a few songs) which showed how good television could be when it was put in the hands of people who knew how to use it to the performers'—and the viewers'—advantage. Astaire returned the next season with "Another Evening. . ." and later with a third dancing special. All of them were superior television divertissements.

(Above) MUSIC WITH MARY MARTIN: This was the nightcap of a day-night Easter Sunday doubleheader which Mary Martin played in 1959. The afternoon show, aimed at children, was called "Magic with Mary Martin." In the evening Miss Martin performed numbers from her various musicals.

(Top, left) FRANCES LANGFORD PRESENTS: Film was becoming a factor in entertainment specials. In this one Frances Langford appeared with Jerry Colonna (and Bob Hope, Hugh O'Brian, Julie London, Edgar Bergen, and George Sanders).

(Left) H.M.S. PINAFORE: One of several television versions of Gilbert and Sullivan's nautical operetta was this *Omnibus* production, with Cyril Ritchard as Sir Joseph Porter.

(Below) ACCENT ON LOVE: Marge and Gower Champion joined with Louis Jourdan (left), and Ginger Rogers, Mike Nichols, and Elaine May for a 1959 *Pontiac Star Parade*.

(Above) TONIGHT WITH BELAFONTE: The folk singer has limited his television bookings to a few guest appearances and fewer specials of his own, the first of which was *Tonight with Belafonte* (and with Odetta) in 1959.

(Right) STRAWBERRY BLONDE: Janet Blair played a suffragette in this 1959 musical, which also starred David Wayne and Eddie Bracken.

(Bottom, right) MEET ME IN ST. LOUIS: Tab Hunter and Jane Powell were the boy and girl next door. Walter Pidgeon, Myrna Loy, Ed Wynn, and Jeanne Crain also were in the cast.

(Below) THE GENE KELLY SHOW: Kelly has headlined a number of specials. On this one, in 1959, he performed with thirteen-year-old Liza Minnelli (this is a rehearsal shot), plus Carl Sandburg and three European ballerinas.

(Right) THE BIG PARTY: Specials came in big packages in 1959. *The Big Party* was supposed to be a series of fifteen, but an absurd format and sponsor interference pooped *Party* while the season was still young. Each of the ninety-minute specials was supposed to be taking place at someone's house, to which a heterogeneous assortment of celebrities had been "invited" (Eva Gabor was hostess to Carol Channing, Sir John Gielgud and the Benny Goodman Trio; Rock Hudson sprung for Tallulah Bankhead, Sammy Davis, Jr., Mort Sahl, Esther Williams, and Carlos Montoya; and so it went). They all stood around the old piano exchanging relentlessly casual banter written by Goodman Ace and his gaggle of comedy writers, and every few minutes they managed to coax one of the guests into performing his specialty, if he had one. Around this particular piano are Barbara Britton, who kept crashing the parties to recite commercial messages; soprano Patrice Munsel; and Abe Burrows, who was associated in the production of the show.

(Below) FORD STARTIME: This was another big series of specials. It billed itself as "TV's Finest Hour." A few times during the season *Startime* lived up to its billing, but shows like these were more typical: *(bottom, left)* "Cindy's Fella" ("Cinderella" in the Wild West), with Lois Smith, George Gobel, and James Stewart; *(bottom, center)* "Meet Cyd Charisse," a musical revue; and *(bottom, right)* "The Jazz Singer," with Jerry Lewis making like Jolson. *Startime*'s impresario was Hubbell Robinson, long an influential force in television programming. In 1966 he became producer of *ABC Stage '67,* whose prospectus read very much like *Startime*'s.

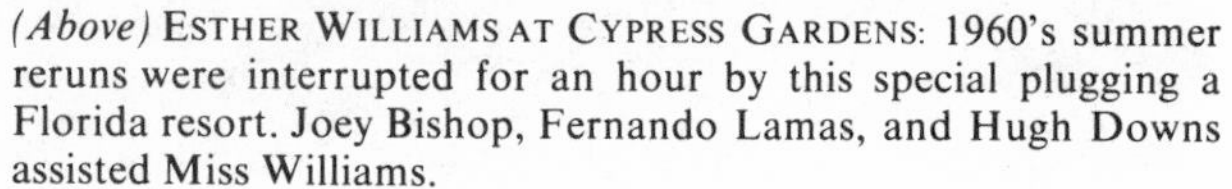

(Above) Esther Williams at Cypress Gardens: 1960's summer reruns were interrupted for an hour by this special plugging a Florida resort. Joey Bishop, Fernando Lamas, and Hugh Downs assisted Miss Williams.

(Top, right) Hollywood Sings: Tammy Grimes and Eddie Albert were joined by Boris Karloff, who sang with them in this 1960 musicale.

(Right) Feathertop: A 1961 musical, with Jane Powell and Hugh O'Brian.

(Below) The Fabulous Fifties: The sixties opened with a nostalgic two-hour salute to the previous decade, produced by the man they always seem to hire for television's most grandiose enterprises, Leland Hayward. He assembled an impressive cast—Rex Harrison and Julie Andrews (here simulating "My Fair Lady" rehearsals), Jackie Gleason, Dick Van Dyke, Nichols and May, Comden and Green, Shelley Berman, Suzy Parker, Eric Sevareid, and, as host, Henry Fonda.

(Top, left) HENRY FONDA AND THE FAMILY: This was "a satiric look at the American family," with Carol Lynley, Dick Van Dyke, and Cara Williams among the lookers.

(Above) THE GOOD YEARS: Fonda again, this time reminiscing about life in America from 1900 to 1914. Lucille Ball, Mort Sahl, and Margaret Hamilton were also involved in this 1961 Leland Hayward show.

(Left) YVES MONTAND ON BROADWAY: Montand was aided by Polly Bergen, John Raitt, Helen Gallagher, and Bobby Van in this musical revue.

(Below) MARINELAND CARNIVAL: These fun-with-fish spectacles are aired annually. Bill ("Jose Jimenez") Dana, Lloyd Bridges, and Rosemary Clooney were in the 1962 edition.

JULIE AND CAROL AT CARNEGIE HALL: All it had was Carol Burnett (left) and Julie Andrews, singing, dancing, and clowning (with an occasional assist from twenty chorus boys) on the stage of Carnegie Hall. It was enough. As good as the Misses Andrews and Burnett were alone, they were even better together in this 1962 show. The result was one of television's fastest-flying hours. Producer Bob Banner, director Joe Hamilton, and writers Mike Nichols and Ken Welch gave the girls plenty to work with.

(Right) ELIZABETH TAYLOR IN LONDON: In 1963 a couple of enterprising producers found a foolproof formula for television specials: hire a movie queen, set her down in a foreign city, and let her guide a tour through the town. It worked first with Elizabeth Taylor.

(Bottom, right) SOPHIA LOREN'S ROME: A year later it scored again with Sophia Loren. (And subsequently Melina Mercouri showed us Greece, and Inger Stevens Sweden.)

(Below) THE BEATLES IN AMERICA: In 1964 they switched things around. Instead of a cinema beauty, they turned their cameras on the four hottest items on the pop-music scene. And instead of unleashing them in Europe, they imported them from there to here. The result was this chronicle of The Beatles' first visit to these shores. Here they gambol in the surf at Miami Beach.

(Left) The Julie Andrews Special: That supercalifragilistic girl was back again in 1965, joined by Gene Kelly for a zingy hour.

(Left, center) The Mikado: NET, the headquarters of educational television, did its share to keep sophisticated entertainment in style on the air. This is John Holmes in a *Festival of the Arts* production of the Gilbert and Sullivan classic, performed by the Sadler's Wells Opera Company and shown on educational stations throughout the United States.

(Bottom, left) Dynamite Tonight: NET also showcased domestic talent. This is a scene from a savagely satiric "actors' opera," with Eugene Troobnick and Bill Redfield.

(Below) Mary Martin at Easter Time: The hardiest perennial of the television-specials circuit turned up again in a 1966 musicale staged by Gower Champion.

MY NAME IS BARBRA:
By 1965 Barbra Streisand had conquered Broadway (in "Funny Girl"), and her records were selling everywhere like bagels sell in Brooklyn, the land of her birth twenty-two years earlier. It took her exactly one hour to add television to her list of conquests. She did a one-woman show, tastefully mounted by Joe Layton and Dwight Hemion, which was the most generously praised special of the 1964–65 season. The next season she did it again, with a new solo special titled "Color Me Barbra." These photos were shot at Bergdorf Goodman during the taping of a sequence for the first show.

(Left) AWARD SHOWS: Many awards are bestowed in television specials every season. The annual Oscar telecast is the biggest of the award shows. The most unpredictable, however, is the Emmy show, in which the television industry passes out statuettes to its own members—and often manages to make a fool of itself through the gaucheries of its show and the absurdities of its award categories. Sammy Davis, Jr. was co-host (with Danny Thomas) of the 1965 Emmy show, which was boycotted by two networks and was an embarrassing muddle from beginning to end.

(Below, left) PARADES: Throughout television history some types of specials have overcome the vagaries of viewers' tastes and proved popular year in and year out—parades, for example. This is Times Square during a Macy's Parade, telecast nationally every Thanksgiving Day.

(Below) TELETHONS: These grueling television marathons, which raised money for charity, were intriguing novelties during the early years. Performers like Dennis James and Jane Pickens (manning the phones and microphones here) participated in many of them, in cities all over the United States.

THE MISS AMERICA PAGEANT:
This annual competition has been making a television spectacle of itself ever since 1954, when it was telecast nationally for the first time. It always attracts one of the largest television audiences of the season. Year by year the show has become slicker—the girls better prepared, the production more polished. This has robbed the Pageant of some of its intrinsic appeal, but one vital element has remained unchanged: Bert Parks, the show's irrepressibly bouncy master of ceremonies, whose fervent rendition of "There she is, Miss America . . ." is one of the most eagerly awaited and enjoyable events of any television season. Here he serenades Marilyn Van Derbur, Miss America 1958, who went on to a television career of her own.

PHILCO-GOODYEAR TELEVISION PLAYHOUSE: Its name changed from week to week, along with its sponsors, but whatever it was called, this Sunday-night series blazed a trail for television drama, and its influence—embodied in the writers, directors, and actors who learned their crafts during *Playhouse's* pioneering days—is still being felt. The show's guiding spirit was its young producer, Fred Coe, seen here with Jose Ferrer, who starred in "Cyrano de Bergerac" on *Playhouse*. The Ferrers and Cyranos had a place in Coe's scheme of things, but new talents and original plays were what gave the series its excitement. Coe sought and found young writers; he encouraged them, coddled them, prodded them, gave them freedom to write their own way; and he produced their plays. Paddy Chayefsky, Tad Mosel, Robert Alan Aurthur, Horton Foote, N. Richard Nash, J. P. Miller, Sumner Locke Elliot, David Shaw, Gore Vidal, Calder Willingham—these men, and others, wrote for *Philco-Goodyear,* and they gave television some of its finest hours.

OCTOBER STORY: *Philco Television Playhouse* began on October 3, 1948. Three years later *Goodyear* started. The first *Goodyear* production, "October Story," starred two of the busiest television actors of that era—Julie Harris and Leslie Nielsen. The entire show was live, of course, and for this scene a camera was placed atop the RCA Building.

MARTY: What was the single outstanding television drama of all time? Most people would answer, "Marty." But while millions have vivid memories of the later movie version, only a handful can recall the original 1953 television drama. The stars of Paddy Chayefsky's play were Rod Steiger, as the nebbish butcher, Marty; and Nancy Marchand, as the girl who brings love into his drab life. Delbert Mann directed both television and film versions of the play.

(Above) Wish on the Moon: Eva Marie Saint (left) and Phyllis Kirk were among those who could be seen frequently in *Philco-Goodyear* dramas like this one.

(Top, right) My Lost Saints: Lili Darvas and Eileen Heckart appeared together in this Tad Mosel play.

(Below) Old Tasselfoot: E. G. Marshall was virtually unknown beyond Broadway when he played a blacksmith in J. P. Miller's drama.

(Bottom, right) The Expendable House: John Cassavetes was virtually unknown *anywhere* until he made a name for himself in early television dramas. Glenda Farrell is with him in this scene from a 1955 play by Reginald Rose.